Praise for
Behind the Counse

"As someone who was [obscured by stamp] material, I found that the lessons students reveal in t[his book echo what I had to learn] on my own over a longer period of time. Th[is] work is about the truth so many students discovered in their efforts to successfully get through high school. They leave a simple path for their peers to follow yet, as their stories reveal, it takes some courage and the willingness to make difficult choices. This is a great resource for students!"

—William Steele, PsyD, MSW, MA
Founder of The National Institute for Trauma and Loss in Children

"*Behind the Counselor's Door* is powerful and eye-opening! It provides the reader with a realistic look and gripping stories of the emotional turmoil that teenagers face and have to deal with from the perspective of a high school counselor. Kuczynski takes a unique approach that enables the reader to find the grit and resiliency to overcome personal challenges and achieve greatness."

—Dave Pelzer
Author of *New York Times* bestseller *A Child Called "It"*
and recipient of The National Jefferson Award

"This book is real, relevant, and reliable! I am thankful for how it will excel my working with teenagers as I plan to provide it to thousands of students. If you're a student, this is a must-read to help navigate life. Adults, this book will inspire you to help students persevere through trials."

—E. J. Swanson
Nationally recognized speaker and author to students

"*Behind the Counselor's Door* is a powerful book that moves beyond problems and focuses on solutions. It encourages teens to develop and strengthen their ability to succeed and make their lives satisfying despite all the challenges they may face. This is a must-read for teens, their parents, and all those who care about them."

—Jerry Moe, MA
National Director of Children's Programs, Betty Ford Center

BEHIND THE COUNSELOR'S DOOR

TEENAGERS' TRUE CONFESSIONS, TRIALS, AND TRIUMPHS

KEVIN KUCZYNSKI

Health Communications, Inc.
Deerfield Beach, Florida

www.hcibooks.com

Library of Congress Cataloging-in-Publication Data
is available through the Library of Congress

© 2015 Kevin Kuczynski

ISBN-13: 978-07573-1841-2 (Paperback)
ISBN-10: 07573-1841-X (Paperback)
ISBN-13: 978-07573-1842-9 (ePub)
ISBN-10: 07573-1842-8 (ePub)

Publisher: Health Communications, Inc.
       3201 S.W. 15th Street
       Deerfield Beach, FL 33442–8190

Cover photo: Kuczynski family photo by Mirela Manea Photography
Cover design by Larissa Hise Henoch
Interior design and formatting by Lawna Patterson Oldfield

This book is dedicated to
my wife, Jennifer, and my children,
Hannah and Ty, who have always supported
this dream of mine. You mean the world to me and
I am a better husband and dad because of you.
Thank you for supporting all of my
late nights of writing. May you aspire to
greatness and make your dreams
become reality.

CONTENTS

Part II: LIFE

PART III: TIPS TO SUCCEED

ACKNOWLEDGMENTS

It's not an understatement to say that writing a book has been one of the most challenging, exhilarating, and rewarding experiences of my life. I could not have achieved what you hold in your hands without supportive people who believed in this project and helped make this dream of mine a reality. To those who have collaborated with me on this journey, thank you. Words cannot express my appreciation for your role in this process. I am indebted to you for your kindness and generosity, as well as for your expertise and professionalism. My greatest desire is that this book is worthy of the time you have invested in this project because of our unified goal to inspire teenagers to believe in themselves, take personal responsibility, and achieve the greatness they are capable of attaining.

Special thanks to:

Nancy Buyle
Robert U. Davidson
Arlene Hallberg
Dr. Kimberly M. Jeszke
Diane Lukas
Jerry Moe

❧

In particular, I'd like to thank my editor Christine Belleris. The role of editors is often unseen. The spotlight is usually on authors, yet, as I came to understand through the process of writing this book, their fingerprints are all over the finished product held by the reader.

Christine, I am privileged to call you my editor and friend. You are truly exceptional and your support of this project is beyond words. I would never have made it through this journey without your unwavering support and expertise. This book has been fine-tuned and reworked with your hand guiding the process. Your imprint is on this book and it is so much better because of it! Thank you!

PREFACE

My position as a school counselor is something I take great pride in. I value the profession and the opportunity we have to work with students and help them navigate through high school as they plan for a life of becoming positive members of society.

One of the reasons I wrote this book is to clarify what counselors deal with behind closed doors. School counselors are vital to the success of schools, but our numbers have experienced a decline in this era of budgetary belt-tightening and cutbacks. It's important to understand how counselors keep schools running smoothly. Teachers become the priority when discussing school effectiveness; however, I want the role and value of the counselor to be recognized for what the profession accomplishes to aid student achievement. In my position, I see the wide variety of issues that teenagers deal with every day. There are hardships at home, the challenges of dating, and struggles with academic success. The temptations of drugs and alcohol are real and occur frequently. We as a society must deal with teenagers and their issues honestly and openly instead of avoiding them as if they don't exist.

Many people see a school counselor as one who falls in a chasm between administrator and teacher, and are unclear about what we actually do. Because of this, the counselor sometimes becomes an afterthought to student success, instead of a catalyst to aid a student in moving forward, both in school and in life.

School counselors serve a critical function to the success of schools beyond scheduling, standardized tests, college/career planning, and crisis counseling. A key role is acting as the avenue that allows students to work through their social/emotional issues (some more critical than others) in an effort to aid them in achieving academic success.

The truth is, sometimes teenagers are not able to work through the complex issues of a problem by themselves. So these problems pile up, causing students to become frustrated, depressed, confused, or deprived of sleep, which can lead to a lack of focus in class, an inability to concentrate, and an apathetic attitude about school work.

School counselors can help teenagers work through their issues, and/or refer them to an appropriate community resource or counseling center for further support. School counselors want students to have a positive, memorable high school experience. I encourage teenagers to get to know their school counselor and recognize that they are there to help them navigate life. Behind the closed door of a school counselor's office can be an empathic person who is willing to listen. Seek them out and experience the comfort and support they can provide.

I came from a professional private-practice background in counseling. I truly enjoyed parts of this field, but the one thing that caused me to leave was the fact that my role in a private practice therapeutic setting was reactionary. The counseling that I had to carry out was intense and lengthy because the "damage" had already been done to the client. I realized that I wanted to take a more proactive role in helping today's teenagers. I believed that if I worked with students as problems arose, I could help them work through these struggles to minimize both the impact of the struggle on their life as well as decrease the amount of time it would take for the intervention to be successful.

Teenagers are the future of our communities. They are tomorrow's police officers, firefighters, doctors, and city officials, among others. The society that we currently live in is sometimes not a conducive environment for them to be positive contributors to society. The issues and circumstances that come to my office each day are a testament to that. So many of the teenagers that I have worked with over the years have parents who divorced, have drug and alcohol problems, or who are just people who expect little of themselves. This leads to these students making poor choices related to school, as well as engaging in self-destructive behaviors, both alone and with their peers outside of school. As time passes and poor choices escalate, I have seen this lead to issues with drugs, alcohol, sexual promiscuity, and in some instances trouble with the law. The best way to get rid of criminals is to stop raising them. We must invest in our teenagers to benefit our society. We must be proactive. We cannot wait.

> The best way to get rid of criminals is to stop raising them.

Frequently, communities invest a large portion of their tax dollars to build more jails and add more police, when the reality is that we need to invest in the family, providing opportunities for communication, to foster a more stable, healthy family unit.

The problem is not society; *we* are society. We are a part of what makes society what it is and we need to be responsible for

> The problem is not society; *we* are society. We are a part of what makes society what it is and we need to be responsible for changing it. We must look at ourselves as the solution and not as contributors to the problem.

changing it. We must look at ourselves as the solution and not as contributors to the problem. If teenagers are going to be profitable individuals who benefit society, we must invest in them. Teenagers can be difference makers.

Contrary to popular opinion, there is so much good that exists among high school students. I have witnessed this many times as I've helped teenagers reach their academic goals to attend college. Additionally, I have also seen my students work through many personal issues that they have avoided for years. My office has been a safe place for kids to share both their triumphs and struggles. The local TV news is always at the ready to broadcast stories of murder, a drug overdose, a shooting, or domestic abuse. Too often the poor choices of teenagers gain press coverage because it offers the viewer shock value. We must begin to broadcast the good in our youth, recognizing that so many teenagers are incredible individuals who do so much in their communities.

> We must provide teenagers with the boundaries that will guide them to a life of success. Life is complicated and teenagers need direction.

We must be a community that allows for communication and dialogue. At times we forget that teenagers are still kids and we live in a world filled with numerous temptations that can lead them astray. We must be the catalyst that stops them from continuing down the wrong path. We must provide teenagers with the boundaries that will guide them to a life of success. Life is complicated and teenagers need direction.

INTRODUCTION

If the walls of my office could talk they would have much to say. In my years of school counseling, I have had more than 25,000 interactions with teenagers, in various roles. But what I enjoy most is working with students individually behind the closed door of my office. My office walls have witnessed dramas both big and small, filled with joy and sorrow, and all-encompassing to the students they've affected. There have been arguments, some between parents and their children, others between students who were so-called "best friends" and had a falling out. Many of these started calmly but nearly ended in fist fights.

I've helped students cope with a friend's suicide, the loss of a family member, a parent's job loss, a divorce, and—more commonly as the economy weakened—the loss of a home due to foreclosure.

I've had students who had a sexual encounter they regret, or were in an abusive relationship where they felt trapped and couldn't find a way to escape. I have had pregnant seniors on the verge of graduation, and pregnant ninth-graders. There were others who partied too hard on the weekend and didn't remember what took place, and those with full-blown substance abuse addiction. I've seen students struggling with self-mutilation and eating disorders. I've made numerous referrals to child protective services, provided

1

food resources for students who had none, and even had students leave school because they got married over the summer.

I've also witnessed the joy of those who celebrate that they are graduating and the sadness of those who have finally come to terms with the fact that they cannot walk with their class because of failed courses. There have been tears of happiness, joy, and laughter as students realize how far they have come in four years.

Of the thousands of students I've worked with over the years, many faced problems or personal issues. Sometimes, a school-related concern is actually a home issue or family problem. In spite of the poor choices made by many students I've worked with, I have also had the privilege and honor of working with numerous exceptional teenagers who chose the right path. Some students rise to the top because they are just good kids with great parents and a strong and supportive family unit, while others have had to overcome extreme family and personal issues to become success stories that inspire us all. Teenagers who achieve greatness are not swallowed up by their trials and tribulations. They choose to overcome adversity. They want better for themselves. They flourish instead of flounder; excel instead of crumble. They achieve success by firmly committing to a goal and renewing their desire each day to work and attain it. This success could be with family or friends, in education and career, or any other goal set by someone who works hard to achieve it.

> Teenagers who achieve greatness are not swallowed up by their trials and tribulations. They choose to overcome adversity.

It's a privilege to learn from these students and an honor to impart guidance to them. After talking with many of these teenagers over the years, I wanted to examine what made them so amazing, and why they have such a strong desire to excel, never being content to settle for mediocre results in life.

What makes these kids yearn for success when others are apathetic? The level of resiliency varies from person to person, but what I find in speaking with these students is that they make a choice to achieve greatness, to be successful. Like them, you must want something better for your life, and then work hard to achieve it while not making excuses for a lack of success.

Your choices determine the path you take in life. You either make choices that lead you down a path of disappointment and setback, or one toward excellence and prominence. Obstacles and hardships that arise may be out of your control. But you *can* control how you respond to them.

> Your choices determine the path you take in life. You either make choices that lead you down a path of disappointment and setback, or one toward excellence and prominence. Obstacles and hardships that arise may be out of your control. But you *can* control how you respond to them.

The stories and lessons in this book are the result of numerous sessions with students and their families: their pain, anger, and tears, as well as their successes, triumphs, and victories. Some students came from strong and united families while others lacked any consistent parental involvement. The sum of these interactions has given me perspective to help teenagers work through their heartache, and I hope it can help you, too.

Society tells us not to feel because if one does not feel one cannot be hurt. In my opinion this could not be more wrong. My students have been willing to open wounds and share their feelings and heartaches. This has allowed me to help them cope, through anger and often tears, as they process much of the baggage they carry. I am a better counselor, coworker, friend, husband, and father because my students have been so gracious over the years to trust, confide, and share with me some of the deepest darkest hurts—and joys—in their lives. I have truly been honored by those who have opened their hearts and lives to me. I am humbled by the genuine willingness of my students to let me help them by working through the struggles in their life, and guiding them on their journey.

If these office walls could talk they would offer insight, direction, and purpose. The students who came to my office were often at a crossroads. Some students desired to achieve greatness, while others floundered due to apathy and a lack of desire for personal excellence. For some, the choice was their own; for others, an extenuating circumstance led them down a path that was not their choosing; for still others, their lack of maturity, experience, and coping skills made them give up.

Some students may never visit their school counselor; others might not even *have* a trained school counselor. Even if you never set foot in a counselor's office, my desire is to open the door to show you what takes place, and to communicate the lessons learned from my students to encourage you to be personally responsible for your level of success in life, and to achieve it no matter what circumstances may impede you on your journey from adolescence to adulthood.

While the experiences in this book are from my students, the issues and the lessons are universal and timeless. The book is in three parts: School, Life, and Tips to Succeed. It covers virtually everything high school students may face, from considering community service, to grief and loss, dating and sex, friendships, college and career planning, and so much more. I write about my students' experiences to inspire you to:

- **Always strive to do the right thing even when it's not easy;**
- **Take each moment as exactly that;**
- **Make choices that allow you to live with passion and purpose instead of missteps and regrets.**

I am hopeful that you will see the value in having a strong work ethic, a passion to succeed, and an awareness of the world around you. These characteristics will serve you well throughout life, and can lead you to excel in school, relationships, and a career. I don't claim to know it all or have all of the answers, but—through the lives of thousands of students—I have witnessed teenagers making choices and later dealing with the consequences of those choices for the rest of their lives.

The journeys on these pages both begin and end with choices. What I have found is that if you want your life to be a success, you must have purpose, values, and morals to help shape the choices you make. It becomes very difficult to make positive choices that propel you forward for the good of yourself and those around you if you don't have strong moral standards guiding those choices. Your morals and values are what keep you accountable when temptation enters your world and encourages you to do otherwise. They become the framework you use to make decisions. Making wise and healthy choices in all areas of your life (academics,

The journeys on these pages both begin and end with choices. What I have found is that if you want your life to be a success, you must have purpose, values, and morals to help shape the choices you make.

relationships, what you watch, what you listen to, how you prioritize your time, etc.) will help you achieve your goals.

This book includes stories about situations that most teenagers can relate to. It is intended to be an opportunity for awareness and a resource to do a self-check of one's motives and ambitions. The pages that follow are an honest (sometimes even blunt) look at how teenagers can take personal responsibility and not just survive high school, but thrive.

My hope is that you will learn from reading about your peers so you can know how to deal with key issues in your lives *before* they occur, thus helping you make better decisions today to improve your tomorrows. I want to shed some light on adolescent issues that need to be discussed more openly at home. I intend to incorporate my own thoughts and perspectives through the trials, triumphs, and tribulations of my students. The students I write about have since graduated, many of them years ago, but they had an impact on my life and I trust they will leave an imprint on you.

It seems many teenagers wander around just existing instead of living. They appear confused and bewildered, lacking the maturity to remain focused on the task or goal in front of them. They don't seem to have a purpose. Lacking any concrete direction, some young people simply live for the moment regardless of the ramifications or consequences. Empowering these teenagers to challenge and ultimately change this thinking is something that I strive for every day as a high school counselor.

I am here, the lights are on, and the first student has just arrived and sat down. Please come in as we step into the office of a high school counselor and go behind closed doors. . . .

Part I

SCHOOL

Please be aware that the names of students that follow
have been changed and alterations have been made to the
details of their stories in an effort to protect their identities.

Chapter 1

ATTENDANCE

I n Michigan, where I work, a new school year begins the first Tuesday after Labor Day. It signals a fresh start for students as well as their parents. I always hope that each year is a building experience—that lessons learned from the previous year can be applied for success in the year ahead.

On the surface, coming to school every day seems like a simple task: get up, get dressed, have breakfast, walk out the door to school. Yet it is often one that becomes minimized and compromised because of the turmoil, dysfunction, and lack of communication that makes many home situations difficult to deal with. I believe the first day of the school year is the most important. It's the first day of more than 180 school days that sets both the standard and the expectation for what is to follow. In the days that follow the first week, teachers explain policies and procedures, strive to learn students' names, and make generalized conclusions (through assessments and evaluations) on student strengths and weaknesses. They assess the abilities of their students and in turn develop curriculum through lesson plans incorporating differentiated instruction.

Behind closed doors, almost every day I deal with students who struggle with the problem of attendance and how it impacts academic performance. Missing the first day of school, especially, starts a student's new school year off on a negative note. Unless you are ill, don't let this be you, because it encourages or reinforces a lazy approach to academics. You might say, "I only go to school because I have to." Remember, school attendance laws are there for a good reason: to keep you accountable so you can become a productive member of society.

> Missing the first day of school, especially, starts a student's new school year off on a negative note.

> Remember, school attendance laws are there for a good reason: to keep you accountable so you can become a productive member of society.

In many countries around the world, students literally get up in the dark and walk for miles for the privilege of learning. Some leave home entirely and live at a boarding school in the hope of giving their families a chance at a better future. Still other children—notably girls—are *prohibited* from going to school at all, and risk their lives by studying in secret. Do you attend school because you *have* to, or do you attend school because you *want* to learn? An apathetic approach to school attendance is a key indicator of your potential for success in the future.

Accepting that it is okay to stay home or skip school because you just don't feel like going, don't like your teachers, or simply don't understand the importance, can snowball into many absences and lead you down a dangerous path toward not graduating due to missing credits, or even dropping out entirely. Teenagers who drop out of school struggle to find a decent paying job of any kind. Think about it: if you were an employer, would you take a chance and hire someone without knowledge and skills, or a responsible history of showing up every day? The "real world" is a lot more demanding, and far less forgiving, than the school environment.

Students who drop out often get into mischievous—sometimes criminal—behavior, and ensuing legal issues. These

> The "real world" is a lot more demanding, and far less forgiving, than the school environment.

young people believe they have nothing more productive to do with their time. Lacking a clear vision, they essentially sabotage their future for the "fun" of immediate gratification.

BRITTANY

And You Thought I Just Didn't Want to Come to School

Brittany was in my office numerous times related to many complex issues, attendance being one of them. Often, students don't come to school because they know they can get away with it. They have no parental accountability and therefore no consequences at home for not attending. Brittany was one of them. From working with many students who have poor attendance, I've observed that not coming to school is almost always a symptom of another issue, usually a problem at home. I have often found that counseling is most effective when the counselor does more listening than

> Not coming to school is almost always a symptom of another issue, usually a problem at home.

talking. Letting a student share his or her heart allows me to listen to their story and pick up on clues. These clues result in me finding out what is contributing to or causing a lack of school attendance. A big clue with Brittany was when she shared that she did not have a healthy relationship with her mother. Although it might not seem like it to parents sometimes, teenagers want and need to have a relationship with them. They just have a difficult time verbalizing it. This turned out to be a major issue in Brittany's life. She wanted what other teenage girls had: to go to the mall, to sit and talk about "real" things that matter in life with her mother.

Brittany's home life was not ideal, to say the least, and Brittany used skipping school as a means to escape from that reality. She didn't run away from home, but instead ran from her responsibilities. Her grades floundered, but her parents didn't care enough about their daughter to care about her grades. Without parental guidance, Brittany made poor choices over and over again, which only compounded her problems.

One of Brittany's poor choices involved seeking security from boyfriends. Brittany felt she had to sleep with a guy in order for him to care about her, but when the sex stopped he left. This false sense of security led her to continually feel used and "dirty." The attention she got was superficial, and the pattern continued. One guy would leave her and she would be on a quest to find a new guy, and with him the love and security she so desperately wanted.

Brittany got to a point where she did not care about anything, including school. Because of this, her attendance deteriorated and it came to my attention. Because of her flawed perspective of self and the lack of parental support at home, school had no value for her.

Brittany and I spent many hours together in an attempt to work through her home life and her relationship with her mother. Brittany now attends school on a regular basis. She still may have setbacks, but her attendance is no longer the issue that it once was. She and I worked through many personal issues. The most critical starting point was that Brittany had to learn to accept the fact that she could only work on what she could control. This was a critical step for her because if she could not come to this conclusion, she would be trapped; her individual success could only be achieved through the support of her mother, which we both knew was not going to happen. She had to accept the fact that she could not change her mother. She could not make her mother care about her, let alone love her and have a relationship with her. Beyond the relationship with her mom we continued to focus on what she *could* control, which was how she viewed herself.

> Brittany had to learn to accept the fact that she could only work on what she could control.

I have often asked my students what they plan on doing after they graduate. Some of them have absolutely no idea and Brittany was one of those students. She had no plans for the future. She was too caught up in conflict at home with her mother and her so-called security through promiscuity. Without a vision for the road ahead and a direction in which to chart your course, it's hard to see the value or importance of school.

> Without a vision for the road ahead and a direction in which to chart your course, it's hard to see the value or importance of school.

I successfully worked with Brittany to develop a plan for the future based on her interests, her talents, and her abilities. With a new sense of purpose and a fresh perspective, she found value in school and set a goal to attend community college. She realized that school was the bridge to achieving her dreams.

Sadly, Brittany's situation is not uncommon. Skipping school becomes an escape, a way to try and avoid a bad situation at home. However, missing school only causes more problems, both for students and for teachers who must invest additional time to help a student catch up. Students who are apathetic about attending (that is, they don't feel like coming) are not high on the priority list when there are others who have real needs for extra help from school personnel due to illness or special circumstances.

> Attending high school is not like taking a correspondence course or participating in an online learning program; you *must* attend school in order to do well.

Attending high school is not like taking a correspondence course or participating in an online learning program; you *must* attend school in order to do well. There is no substitute for showing up every day and paying attention. True learning is accomplished through understanding new material, presented by a teacher interacting with a classroom of students. While online/virtual courses serve a purpose—and are required as part of the curriculum in some states—they cannot replicate this kind of interaction! Learning is part knowledge and part social. It is the vehicle that drives each student toward their future aspirations. It allows you to interact with your teacher and enhance your social skills by working with peers. This helps you learn how to make it in today's demanding workplace, where people must interact in group situations day in and day out.

Parents need to be responsible to get their children to school each and every day. However, students, you must do your part. You know you need to attend school ready to learn every day even if there are times when you would rather stay home. Think of it this way: your career dreams are the big prize. To boost your chances of "winning" the prize, you need to put more raffle tickets in the jar. Each day that you attend school is like buying another ticket, and bettering your odds of having the life you want. Unlike a raffle, however, no luck is involved—just work and dedication. So attend school—don't throw away your chance to make your dreams a reality.

POINTS TO PONDER . . .

✔ Many students who do not attend school on a regular basis often have an underlying struggle that keeps them from attending.

✔ School is your bridge to a successful future.

✔ You must attend school in order to succeed academically.

✔ Do you attend school because you have to or because you want to?

✔ You will only get out of school what you put into it. Are you trying your best?

✔ If you don't have a vision for the future, some sort of direction as to where you want to go, it is hard to set goals along the way to make that vision become reality. As the old adage goes, if you don't chart a course for your ship, the ship will take you where it wants to go. What is your vision for your future?

✔ What is keeping you from attending school? Talk to an adult, teacher, or school counselor to get help.

Chapter 2

HOMEWORK

I f I had to pick one school issue that takes up the majority of my day, it would be homework. I call students to my office on a daily basis to deal with this. Some students come to me because they feel their homework is too hard, or they don't understand it, or they are frustrated because they just don't think they will ever use the information so they don't want to bother learning it. Numerous parents call me to discuss their child's inability or refusal to complete homework as well. Most parents do this to communicate with the teacher in an effort to help their child's learning, while others may complain about the amount of homework or the teacher's style of educating.

Homework is much more than filling in blanks on a worksheet. In my office, the subject of homework leads me to confront students about who they are and what they want. School attendance is one ticket to a student's future success, and homework is the other. Not only do you need to show up and pay attention, but you also must do the assigned work after school to demonstrate you understand what you just spent several hours learning. The homework a student completes shows both who they are as a person, and what they want in life. How hard a student is willing to work shows how much the student wants to achieve in the future. It allows them to fulfill the vision they have for their life and, as with most everything, doing homework—or not doing it—is a choice.

> The homework a student completes shows both who they are as a person, and what they want in life.

Behind my closed door, things get interesting. One day, I received an email from a parent. He attached a story that had been given to him. It was his way of expressing to me the love he has for his son, but also the frustration he has for his son's poor school performance. It spoke to the impact that homework and grades have on both the parent as well as the teenager.

In this story a father was walking through his home when, surprisingly, he noticed that his son's bedroom was clean. To his astonishment his son's clothes were all picked up off the floor and the clean clothes had been not only neatly folded but placed in the appropriate dresser drawer. Video games were organized and his desk was clean to the point that now it could actually be used as a place to do school work. The father saw that the carpet had been vacuumed and the trash had been removed. He then noticed the bed perfectly made, like in a hotel room. Upon further examination he noticed an envelope carefully placed on the bed with "Dad" clearly written on it. With great apprehension the man opened the envelope. The letter read as follows:

Dad,

    It is with overwhelming regret and sadness that I am writing to you now. I had to elope with my girlfriend because I wanted to avoid a scene with you and Mom.

    I've been finding real passion with Stacy and she is so nice. But I knew you would not approve of her because of all of her piercings, tattoos, tight motorcycle clothes, and the fact that she is much older than I am. But it is not only the passion . . . Dad, she's pregnant. If you could share this with Mom I would appreciate it.

    Stacy said that we will be very happy. She owns a trailer in the woods of West Virginia and has stacked enough firewood to get us through the winter. We share a dream of having many more children together.

    Stacy has opened my eyes to the fact that marijuana doesn't really hurt anyone. We will be growing it for ourselves and trading it with people who live near us for cocaine, ecstasy, and some food as well. In the meantime we pray that science will find a cure for hepatitis C so Stacy can get better.

    Don't worry Dad. I'm 15 years old and I know how to take care of myself. Someday I'm sure we will come back and visit so you can get to know Stacy and your grandchildren.

Love,

Your son Robert

    P.S. Dad, none of the above is true. I'm over at Caleb's house. I just wanted you to know that there are worse things in life than me not doing my homework and my report card that is in my center desk drawer.

    I love you. Call me on my cell when it's safe to come home!!![1]

1 http://www.policyholdersofamerica.org/pdf_public/The_Report_Card.pdf

The story clearly illustrates the great lengths teenagers will go to avoid the consequences of poor grades. Robert is a testament to that. If students such as Robert put that kind of effort into completing the homework necessary to earn better grades, then bad grades wouldn't be the issue. Instead, students could focus on areas of weakness and get tutoring to bring about improved grades.

BRIAN

They Call It Homework for a Reason

I had spoken with Brian on a few occasions and called him down out of his English class to my office one morning, at the request of his assistant principal, because of his consistent lack of effort. I knew that Brian was not happy with me because he complained about me to this assistant principal (I will tell you why later).

Brian and I chatted briefly for a moment or two and then I asked him, "Do you know why I called you down here this morning?"

"I don't know," Brian responded.

"It's about your grades, Brian," I said. "You are still failing two classes and you are six months from graduation. I am not sure if you are going to get there."

"I am trying," he explained to me.

I said, "Brian, you have a 1 percent average in English . . . 1 percent! Are you really trying?" I asked firmly, knowing the answer.

"Yes, I am!" he said.

"Brian, I spoke with your assistant principal. She told me that you were upset with me. She said that I used a term and you were upset that I used this term. Is that correct?" I said.

"Yes," Brian responded.

"What did I say that made you so upset? I saw you a few weeks ago and have not heard anything until yesterday. What is bothering you about our conversation?"

In a frustrated tone Brian replied, "You thought I was lazy."

I asked Brian to look at it from my perspective. "You basically complete no homework, you are failing two classes, you have a 1 percent in English class, and you are not likely to graduate if this continues. What am I supposed to think, do, or say to you?"

Brian simply stated: "I don't know."

Brian was hurt that I called him lazy. Instead of taking responsibility for his poor grades and lack of effort at school, he chose to take charge by striving to "get me in trouble." The problem here is that he wanted to blame *me* for his lack of effort. He wanted to blame *me* for the fact that he was doing *nothing*. He was hoping the attention would be put on *me* by the assistant principal and not on *his* lack of work.

I am amazed at how many kids feel this way. I often tell my students that I will help and support them, but I will not work harder for their grades than they do. There is no substitute for hard work if you want to succeed. Many teenagers put in so much effort avoiding school work, that it would take less effort if they just completed the work and did it well.

> There is no substitute for hard work if you want to succeed.

Teenagers have been raised in a society where they get what they want instantly. Their lives are motivated by convenience. Technology seems to be the driving force behind that. I have often told my students that how you approach homework is an accurate indicator of what you want to get out of your education and how much

> How you approach homework is an accurate indicator of what you want to get out of your education and how much you want to contribute to society in the future.

you want to contribute to society in the future.

Today, all you have to do is type in a couple of words and your research for an essay, speech, or project is right there before you. No effort or dedication is necessary. So I come along as a high school counselor asking teenagers to invest four solid years, the better part of 700 school days, before they graduate. It highlights how much hard work they will have to do on a daily basis to receive a high school diploma. For many students the reward is too far away. Teenagers, your future is determined by the habits that you develop in high school—not in college. The reason I say this is because the habits you develop become a lifestyle. You may be able to change habits, but it is much more difficult to change a lifestyle. I often hear from students how they plan to change once they start college. This sounds great—in theory. The problem is that in college you have no accountability, no one looking over your shoulder keeping an eye on you. The responsibility falls squarely on you. Your college or university will take your money whether you do the work or not. You must develop a drive to want to do better and to excel. Completing your homework is a great indicator of that—and the beginning of a successful habit.

Brian decided to pass the blame on me in an effort to shift the focus from himself. While some students might consider homework a teacher-designed torture method, homework is designed as practice and as a means to help your grade, not hurt it. It prepares you for the tests and quizzes that are to come. Many of you have heard the saying that practice makes perfect, but if no one is perfect, then why practice? Some would say this is a great point, but from my perspective it is misguided. I don't expect perfection; I expect the best quality work you can put out on a daily basis. Practice may not result in you being perfect, but it is the *pursuit* of perfection that should inspire you. Practice creates an ambition to achieve greatness. Even if you don't make it to the pinnacle of greatness, you know you are a lot closer because you aspired to a higher level of excellence in the journey through your schooling.

Brian didn't care enough to practice. He didn't value the knowledge and learning. I'm not saying you should value homework in the manner that I do. This is unrealistic because I have both lived and experienced things different from you. Homework comes down to you valuing it for yourself because you know that it is a stepping stone to future academic (college) and career success. If Brian cared about his future and the direction to get there, he would want to complete homework more successfully.

I have learned that I cannot make a student care about homework, and a parent cannot make a student get the homework done. Sure, a parent can *force* you to do it, but if they do, we both know you will only do it to quiet your parents. I can't make a teenager care. I can't make you, reading this book, care. What I can do is help you see that homework is important. Homework is not fun; if it was fun they would not refer to it as work that is done at home. Homework distinguishes those who want a better future for themselves and are thus willing to sacrifice what they want for themselves today. The pursuit of something better in the future drives those teenagers who are willing to invest in today.

I have found that when students choose not to do homework, they almost always choose not to do it *for a reason*. If you choose to do something in life, you do it for a reason. There is a benefit, a payoff. If you choose to *not* do something, you want to avoid it or because there are other factors that are affecting (or distracting) you.

JORDAN

I've Got Bigger Things to Deal With!

I called Jordan down to my office. I had spoken with him a couple of times about not doing his homework. After numerous attempts to get to the bottom of his avoidance of homework, I asked his parents come in so the four of us could sit down and discuss his situation. Jordan tried not to be part of this meeting; he didn't want to face the reality of his circumstances and wanted to avoid confrontation. His mother arrived and Jordan showed up to my office late, but at least he showed up. We talked about many things related to his struggles, yet I was never able to push the right button to generate a response that would move him forward and focus more on his studies. Because of this I sent Jordan back to class. As he left my office I told him that I would follow up with him in the next few days.

Jordan's mother stayed and we continued to talk. I asked about Jordan's background. She shared with me that she and Jordan's father had divorced when Jordan was in elementary school. She struggled on her own to raise him, then she found a new boyfriend. This man treated her well and he became a father figure and best friend to Jordan. The relationship progressed and she got married, just prior to Jordan beginning high school. She reported that the relationship was great, and that the new stepfather cared so much about Jordan that he adopted him. However, in the last couple of years, his relationship with Jordan had diminished, even though it seemed like the stepfather continued to treat his mom well. Jordan's adoptive father was there, but he never seemed connected or involved anymore. He no longer asked Jordan how his day at school was, stopped attending parent/teacher conferences, and was no longer willing to help him with his homework. He was Jordan's father in title, but not in connection through an honest, authentic relationship.

Jordan's mom asked me what I thought about the situation. I told her that I have found that all kids want two things: they want boundaries and they want attention. No teenager is going to ask for boundaries. They are reaching out with their hands finding their way; boundaries let them know when they have gone too far. In Jordan's case his issue was attention. Jordan longed for attention. Jordan was not getting attention from his father. He seemed to seek it out, but never got it in return. His actions demonstrated that negative attention was better than no attention.

I asked his mother to think about things from her son's perspective for a moment. Jordan didn't get to select his parents. He had to go with what was given to him, and what happened? His parents got divorced and his biological father left him. His father was largely out of the picture and never filled his role as a parent. After the divorce, he only showed up once in a while—generally unannounced—even missing birthdays and holidays. Did Jordan get to decide this? No. Did Jordan even have a say? No. He had to live with the decisions that other people made. I had Mom then fast forward to today. Now he had an adoptive father who picked him. By adopting him, he chose Jordan. His choice was pretty amazing.

Jordan basically was selected to be this man's son. He essentially said: "I want you" and Jordan loved every second of the attention.

My dialogue with Jordan's mother continued as I said, "You said their relationship has soured and he doesn't seem to care about Jordan the way he used to." She nodded her head.

I asked Mom, "Why did Jordan come to the meeting today?"

She responded matter-of-factly, "Because I made him come, because I want him to do better in school and graduate."

I wanted to delve deeper into this, knowing there was more to this story than the obvious, so I responded, "I understand that, but what is another reason as to why Jordan came to this meeting?"

She looked confused and, shaking her head, said, "I don't know."

I continued, "Who didn't come to the meeting today?"

"I don't know, who?" she responded.

I calmly stated, "His dad—make that either dad."

Her bewilderment morphed into irritation and she snapped back by saying, "But I'm here!"

I went on to explain to her that she can give 110 percent of herself to be a parent to Jordan, but it will always only be 50 percent at best. There is no substitute for Jordan's biological and adoptive fathers. Jordan wanted to see if his adoptive father cared enough to come to the meeting.

I said, "As soon as he opened my office door and his father was not there Jordan gained all of the information that mattered to him. His father was invited and knew you were coming to this meeting and still chose not to show up."

Jordan wanted to find out if his dad (biological or adoptive) cared enough about him to attend. Jordan didn't believe he was worthy enough to his father who picked him (chose to adopt him) to show up.

I would later find out that Jordan's mom and adoptive dad argue and fight often and she was contemplating separation and eventual divorce. Jordan saw their conflict played over and over again in the family's living room. For Jordan this was another cycle of a very familiar pattern. Homework for Jordan was a task that fell way down the priority list. Every day after school, he wondered how much arguing was going to take place at home, and whether he was valued enough by *any* parent.

Jordan, like many other teenagers, has obstacles and issues out of his control that prohibit him from making homework a priority. Despite impediments in the lives of students combined with their inability to control their struggles, students can place all of their efforts (and sometimes even anger) into their homework. For some, homework becomes a means to better their future and avoid turmoil at home. They can throw themselves into it determined to show everyone what they are capable of achieving.

> For some, homework becomes a means to better their future and avoid turmoil at home.

In the workplace your employer will expect you to complete tasks related to your job despite personal struggles and family difficulties. It's not that your employer doesn't care about your personal issues. The issue is that your employer needs you to press on and deal with your issues on your own time. Your employer cares; the issue lies in the fact that we all have difficult personal issues and we must overcome them and excel. This same principle applies to school. Students must learn to control what they can to prepare them for the demands of life in the future. One way to develop this control is to complete homework to improve grades. Then you'll see that renewed effort produces results.

EMILY

I Will Succeed, No Matter What!

Homework is what motivated Emily. She was a senior who used homework and school to better herself. Homework motivated her so much so that she left her home school and enrolled at my school, because she thought that there were fewer discipline problems and she would get a better education. Although this seems like a great idea, there were numerous obstacles because she came from a dysfunctional home. She had parents who were divorced. One parent was on disability and the other just did odd jobs and miscellaneous car repairs. She had a dad who was seldom around and an older brother who floundered because he had dropped out of high school. He certainly would not go out of his way to help his sister. As a result, Emily had to find her own ride to school, sometimes with her dad or brother, but most of the time with a friend. Neither her dad nor her brother wanted to get up each morning and take her.

But for Emily, no obstacle was too difficult to overcome. Once at school, she embraced homework, learning, and her future because she knew she could control the outcome. She could control the end result. Emily eliminated excuses, while many students make them prevalent. They seek to use their setbacks and dysfunction as justification for their lack of effort and avoidance of homework. Not Emily. Excuses were replaced with determination. Setbacks were replaced by a work ethic and a passion to succeed.

Homework is an important part of the learning process. It helps you retain more of what you learn. You should do homework to improve your learning and better your future. The issue is a matter of what you want out of life. You have to be willing to invest *in* your life in order to get something *out* of it. Completing your homework every day helps to make that happen. After all, if you don't have the drive to succeed through the basic step of homework completion, other students will pass you by. They will take your place at the college or vocational school you wanted to go to, they will earn the scholarships that had your name on them, and most importantly, these more motivated high school students will take the job and paycheck that were meant to be for you. There goes your successful career. Is that acceptable to you? If not, be inspired by Emily, be focused on your goals, be driven to finish homework and finish it well. Homework is your avenue to a world of opportunities that begins in high school and ultimately lasts a lifetime.

POINTS TO PONDER...

✔ The effort you make when completing homework demonstrates who you are from within and what you want in life.

✔ Nobody should work harder for your grades than you do.

✔ Homework is practice that creates an ambition to achieve greatness in life.

✔ When you do homework, do you do your best or do you settle for "good enough"?

✔ Many teenagers who have family or personal struggles at home invest in their schoolwork because it is their ticket to a brighter future.

✔ If you don't have the drive to achieve through homework, other students will pass you by. They will take your place at college, earn the scholarships that had your name on them, and take the job and paycheck that were meant to be for you. Does this upset or bother you?

✔ Homework is your avenue to a world of opportunity that begins in high school and lasts a lifetime. From where you are right now, what does your future look like?

Chapter 3

HIGH SCHOOL SCHEDULING

After working so closely with students in my role as a school counselor, once they graduate, I have no idea what happens to most of them. Many students e-mail me and still more stop in for a visit, but the large majority of students don't. Of course, I think about them and wonder what happened in the years after they walked across the stage and were awarded their diplomas. Did they go to college? If they did, did they graduate? What university did they transfer to after attending a community college? Where are they working? Did they get a good-paying job?

I set students on a path that culminates with graduation. To get them there, I work with students to help them select classes so they can achieve their academic goals. Each year this process is completed again. With each passing year selecting classes for the next takes more time and thoughtful consideration to complete. It all depends on what college and/or career plans a student is considering.

When you select classes for high school next year, don't choose classes quickly. I encourage you to take your time and think about what classes you would *like* to take, then ask your counselor for suggestions as to what classes you *should* take, based on your college and career plans. High school course selection is serious, and it will go a long way in determining which college you may attend. Colleges have specific admission requirements. Some will require a certain number of core classes, while others may require or prefer a foreign language. The rigor or difficulty of the courses you take can play a role in your admission to college. This must be considered as you select your high school classes, especially as a junior or senior. Colleges look at these years closely to determine what type of student you are.

High school classes are also an opportunity for you to explore a variety of career paths. When you select your elective classes, try something new. A new class may open your eyes to careers you may have not previously considered. Maybe you enjoy art, but you have never considered trying graphic arts or computer animation. You may excel at writing essays, but you never have tried creative writing, or writing an article for the school newspaper. To aid in the scheduling process I have long believed that high school courses (primarily electives) should be taught in alternating years. For example, maybe one year philosophy is offered and it's not the next year because the high school offers anthropology in its place. This gives you as the student more elective courses to choose from, thus allowing you to explore career options on a wider scale. If this option does not exist at your school, pick as many different electives as possible, and then research various careers online that you may find interesting as you seek to continue your education after high school.

I often encourage all students to take four years of the four "cores" (math, English, social studies, and science). I do this because most students will consider some form of college, and most other students can still benefit from the skills learned once they're in the workplace. Additionally, taking these higher level classes as an upperclassman enhances your preparation for college.

I recommend that you choose classes that will challenge you but not overwhelm you. How do you know what will overwhelm you? It is different for every student, but how hard you are willing to work plays a role in determining that. Your daily work ethic shows your commitment level and therefore indicates your level of success in the class. Colleges only see the semester grades of the classes you completed. The appropriate level or difficulty of a course for you can be determined by trying classes in ninth and tenth grade. Attempting to perform at a high level in accelerated or honors courses will let you know if AP courses are appropriate for you in your upperclassman years. Maintaining a high grade-point average is challenging for anyone who takes rigorous courses. AP classes are not what are best for everyone. Take great care in selecting your classes, and seek advice from your parents, teachers, and school counselor.

> Choose classes that will challenge you but not overwhelm you.

As you move into your upperclassman years, the classes you take should be more and more difficult. You should have a lot

> High school courses become preparation for the demands of college. These courses allow you to see what you are capable of academically before you ever step on a college campus.

of homework and studying to do. High school courses become preparation for the demands of college. These courses allow you to see what you are capable of academically before you ever step on a college campus.

I often hear from students that the "switch will flip" when they get to college and they will work hard and take challenging classes then. The odds of this occurring are slim, thus I challenge students to take hard classes now so they are better prepared for college. Many students hope to have a fun and relaxing senior year and want to take easier classes. However, this only causes you to develop poor study habits prior to going to college. It would be like a runner being in top athletic form, then deciding to take it easy on training and going on a doughnut-and-chips meal plan for a year before a marathon.

> The best predictor of future behavior is the past.

You don't just want to get to the starting line, you want to finish the race, and complete it well with a quality result! The best predictor of future behavior is the past. Because of this, if you aren't focused and working hard now in high school you probably won't be when you begin college.

ALLANA

Challenge Yourself to Succeed

Allana was a student of mine who wanted to take easy classes even though she was capable of excelling in more challenging courses. She was a strong student academically, but I was not surprised to find out that she wanted to take the easier English class for her senior year. I wanted her to take the AP Language and Composition class—the harder course. Allana was stubborn, but after much encouragement on my part she agreed to take the more difficult course. As her senior year was concluding, I called her down to reflect on this decision. She arrived just after lunch. I closed the door to my office, and the conversation began.

"So Allana, it is now May and you graduate in just a couple of weeks. Looking back, what are your thoughts about the English class we decided you should take this year?" I asked.

She said, "Well, you know I really didn't want to take it."

"I know that, but what about the course? Do you have any regrets? You did well in it, you got a B+," I answered.

Allana responded, "You know, it wasn't as bad as I thought it would be, but it was a lot of work. Especially writing!"

". . . And I told you before the class started it would be a lot of work," I said.

"You're right," Allana replied.

"Allana, I really want to know what you think. If you did it all over again, would you still take the class?"

She thought about this for a few minutes, then replied, "Honestly, I think I would."

"Okay, why?" I asked.

Allana explained, "I think I would do it again for one reason. I hated all of the reading, but I felt like I really learned how to write, and write well. I needed that. I thought I was a good writer before the class, but taking the class showed me I had a lot to improve upon."

"Can you write well now?" I inquired.

"Yeah, I have always heard that you write a lot in college and now I feel like I am ready for that challenge," she said with a look of accomplishment.

"I am so glad you don't regret taking the class."

"Oh . . . and guess what?" she added. "I feared taking the class because I didn't think I could do well in it. I surprised myself with what I could do."

I said, "Good for you! You see Allana, when you are in a position where you must respond, it is amazing what you can do!"

Allana finished our conversation with words that are music to a guidance counselor's ears, "Yeah, I am definitely more capable than what I thought!"

The classes you choose to take in high school and how hard you work at them will ultimately determine who you become. The classes will shape you as well as the decisions you make for years to come. The grades you get will mold you and the difficulty of the courses selected will help bring into focus the future steps you will take in life.

> The classes you choose to take in high school and how hard you work at them will ultimately determine who you become.

When former students do contact me or I contact them after graduation, our discussions often reflect on their memories of high school and how it prepared them for college. I do this to assess the guidance I provide to students, but also to have students consider the classes they took in high school and how those classes prepared them for their college classes. I have found that I get more honesty from former students when I ask them to do this while they are in their college classes. One of the responses I got back was from Jenna. I found Jenna to be very candid as she had some interesting perspectives for me to consider.

JENNA

If Only I Could Do High School Over Again

Jenna was a quality student when she was in high school. She could have achieved at a much higher level, but she settled for decent grades and never really pushed herself to excel at the highest level possible. She had a B/B+ average when she could have earned straight A's.

Despite this Jenna ended up attending a very well-known university and we have stayed in touch over the years. I asked her to look back at high school and how it prepared her for college. Her response was interesting, and I think it will be valuable to you if, like Jenna, you want to graduate and go on to college. Students often think of getting into college as the end goal, but you also need to consider the workload that will hit you when you get there. Factor in living on your own for the first time, having a block schedule perhaps for the first time, and social pressures. Jenna's comments provide great insight as to what college is like and what you should expect when you get there. Jenna wrote:

In high school teachers teach you; they teach you everything you need to know. At my university they just teach you the basic ideas and expect you to branch off from that. They expect you to explore and investigate in order to learn. College is more about application of information and less about memorizing facts and spitting back information. The facts are important, but you have to go deeper and apply it to situations.

Also in high school your grade can be boosted by homework, so if you do poorly on a test or two the homework is there to save you so you can still get a solid grade despite doing poorly on a few things. In college your grade is like . . . all exams!! There is no homework grade to save you. You must do well on your tests or exams. There are only one or two for the whole class in a semester and however you do on those tests determines your grade for the semester. It varies with each class, but usually the grade is entirely based on a couple of tests.

I definitely feel like my high school and the courses I took prepared me for college. My problem was the study habits that I picked up after high school. In high school I could go to class, pay attention, take notes and do my homework and I could pass with an A. But here in college sometimes I'll spend five hours in the library and still feel like I'm not prepared whatsoever. Much of this is caused by my professors teaching only the basic ideas and I then have to do the work to branch out from it.

Oh! One more thing! As much as I would have hated it . . . I have to say this: English teachers and history teachers should have us writing more essays and they should be grading them a lot harder in order to prepare us for what professors expect in college. That is one of my biggest criticisms. I needed to write more in high school. Professors want you to write in college and they grade the information you write about, they do not want to have to teach you how to write. I honestly would have hated *doing all of that extra writing in high school but it probably would be less difficult for me now if I would have had a better background in it.*

Other than that, college is just a whole different experience that is really hard to prepare for. As much as people tell you what to expect in college, they can help you to a point, but as a student you really don't understand what college and the demands of it are like until you are here.

Hope this helps your students out,

Jenna ☺

Selecting appropriate classes in high school that align with your career aspirations is what is important. If your future career plans require you to further your education, then select classes that would help prepare you for the demands of college. The rate at which students don't graduate from college is much greater than you might think. According to the most current numbers from the National Center for Education Statistics, "The 2012 graduation rate for first-time, full-time undergraduate students who began their pursuit of a bachelor's degree at a four-year degree-granting institution in fall 2006 was 59 percent. That is, 59 percent of first-time, full-time students who began seeking a bachelor's degree at a four-year institution in fall 2006 completed the degree at that institution within six years."[2] Colleges have great results when it comes to enrolling students, but poor results when it comes to those same students graduating.

Your higher education aspirations should not be about being admitted to college, they should be about graduating. You should consider anything short of that unacceptable. There are many reasons why students do not finish college; it could be a lack of work ethic, financial problems, failed classes, or a lack of self-discipline. The reason does not matter. The only issue you need to be concerned about is to make sure that you are not a part of the statistics of students not graduating from college. Go to college, if that is part of your career plans, be disciplined enough to work hard without making excuses, and celebrate your success on the day of your college graduation.

> Your higher education aspirations should not be about being admitted to college, they should be about graduating. You should consider anything short of that unacceptable.

2 http://nces.ed.gov/fastfacts/display.asp?id=40

I recently read an article where an education researcher believes that high school students today *are not* "college material" because they come from low-income homes and lack academic ability; therefore, they are not likely to graduate. Speaking as someone who works with high school students, teenagers like you, every single day, I can boldly state that teenagers today *are* "college material." Every one of you is college material if that is what you choose. However, if college is not for you for whatever reason, consider going to a trade or vocational school. This perspective allows you to grow up with college or a trade school being an expected result after high school. There are a wide variety of jobs that pay well if you further your education through vocational training, such as being an electrician, a veterinary technician, or an auto mechanic. Although I believe you could go to college and have an excellent chance of being successful, attending a trade school is a solid option for growing a successful career.

College preparation begins with a mindset, a perspective. This perspective is what leads to college admissions and ultimately a college diploma. Sure, some of you may have to work harder than others in order to succeed. Some of you may need tutoring, study groups, or remedial classes, but the path to a college graduation is possible. I am tired of people declaring that teenagers aren't good enough or they aren't college material. I want to raise the bar, to raise expectations. Believe that college is possible because it is. You just have to be willing to work hard enough to achieve it. Eliminate the excuses. Have a strong work ethic. I would rather you raise the level of expectations than lower the level of success just so you could reach it a little easier.

The truth is that you can be college material if you choose. The issue of your success in college comes down to hard work (more on this later). How hard are you willing to work? Will you go to tutoring? Will you attend a study group? Will you study for a test earlier than the night before? How badly do you want it? How much do you want to achieve in life? I

> The truth is that you can be college material if you choose.

see it every day. Remember, I work with kids like you all day, every day. They often want to take the easy way out. Is that you? Do you complain about how much homework you have every night? Do you take classes that demand your best? Are you willing to rise above your friends who are content with getting mediocre grades? This is what separates high school students: your level of motivation. I can provide all types of intervention. I can offer tutoring, study sessions, and test prep classes to name a few, but you have to *want* it. You have to want to *achieve*! You have to want to make it! You must desire success! It has to come from within. I can't motivate teenagers to succeed, I can only inspire someone to motivate themselves.

Are you inspired? Are you motivated? Are you motivated enough to bring about change in your life? You know there are lots of people who say what someone wants to hear, but they just can't make that happen. They can't make the needed changes. Can you

> I can't motivate teenagers to succeed, I can only inspire someone to motivate themselves.

make changes in your life? The truth is that our society will always need people to carry out low-paying jobs. If that is not for you, then work hard and plan for college because you can be college material. You can be a difference maker! Yes, *you*!

If this is what you want, begin by taking challenging classes in high school that allow you to explore career options. Thoughtful scheduling during high school with an eye to the future can lead to college because you'll be the college material so many schools are looking for.

POINTS TO PONDER...

✔ Do you put thought into selecting your high school classes each year? Why or why not?

✔ Many students have ability, but don't use it. It's a big problem in our schools. Do you agree? If so, how do we address this issue? How do you address it in your own life?

✔ The only person who can use your abilities is you. Are you using them or wasting them?

✔ What kind of education did your parents have? Did they go to college? Do they value education? How do their views on higher education impact how you look at going to college?

✔ What courses can you take in high school to help you achieve your career/college goals?

✔ Motivated people are the ones who see results and achieve success. Are you a motivated person? If not, what do you need to do to get motivated?

✔ What steps will you take in high school so that you can succeed in college and ultimately in a career?

Chapter 4

COMMUNITY SERVICE

We live in a world filled with greed and selfishness. People often think of themselves first and anyone in need second, if at all. However, our society is only as strong as its weakest link. Life is difficult, and circumstances can change our situation in an instant—everybody needs help at some point in life.

Currently, Maryland is the only state that requires community service as a part of their graduation requirement, although more and more individual school districts are beginning to require it for graduation.[3] Larger school districts including Atlanta, Chicago, and Philadelphia require community service as part of the graduation requirement as do numerous other school districts across the country.

3 http://www.edweek.org/ew/articles/2013/08/21/01volunteer_ep.h33.html ?qs=VOLUNTEERISM.

> Doing something for others gives you confidence and lifts your self-esteem.

Giving back to the community in some way is worthwhile because it makes you feel good knowing that you did something to help someone else. Doing something for others gives you confidence and lifts your self-esteem. You show those you help that there are quality people in a selfish and fallen world. Serving others in need shows that you place value in humanity (people). At the same time, you learn about working with people from different backgrounds. Ways to help support people in need include volunteering in nursing homes, serving in animal shelters, or working with the disadvantaged through food pantries, homeless shelters or programs like Habitat for Humanity.

HAILEY

Your Life Is About More Than You

> Community service is a key indicator of who you are as a person.

Community service is often a key ingredient in a high school senior's college application. I believe community service is a key indicator of who you are as a person. Hailey was one of those students. She was a very driven person. She wanted to do well in school and succeeded as her grade point average placed her at the very top of her class. What was unique about her is that she was only a sophomore. She exhibited forward thinking. Planning for your future is never a bad idea; especially when considering college, because it is such a lengthy process.

I had met Hailey before, but our conversation this time would be different. I was following up with Hailey after a meeting with her parents a couple of days earlier at parent-teacher conferences. My conversation with them centered around the fact that their daughter planned on attending an elite university. Her parents shared with me that they had some viewpoints about her being accepted at elite colleges. Her parents believed that Hailey had an excellent chance of being admitted to the university that interested her when she became a senior because of her grades. However, they were very concerned because all she did was study. Hailey was never involved in any school activities, nor did she participate in any extracurricular activities such as volunteering at her church or completing any community service. Her parents believed this would hinder her chances of going to the elite colleges that interested her. I agreed with their views and we discussed many other things. I told them I would discuss these issues with Hailey and asked that she come into my office.

Hailey came down out of her advanced math class to discuss college and issues related to college acceptance. It is somewhat unusual for a student to discuss higher education issues in November of their sophomore year, but she had been planning for college ever since I first met her in the eighth grade. Hanging up the phone, I motioned for her to come in.

"Hailey, did your parents talk with you about the conversation I had with them at the conferences?" I asked.

Hailey avoided eye contact with me, as if she was thoroughly embarrassed that they had called me. Glumly, she said, "Yes, they told me about it."

I asked her to share what they told her, and Hailey responded, "I found it hard to believe that you thought I might have a tough time getting into the colleges that I am interested in. I work hard and get good grades. In fact, I even do well on practice tests for the ACT."

I said, "Hailey, I hear what you are saying, but let's look at it from another perspective. You are a white, female, middle-class high school student who has a 4.0-plus grade point average. You don't play sports and you are not in band. My point is this: when you are a senior you'll find that there are thousands of other seniors across the country just like you applying for college. Nothing separates you from other applicants. What are your thoughts about community service?"

Hailey responded in a frustrated tone, "My parents probably told you that I have never really done much community service because it just is not 'me.'"

Our conversation continued and Hailey's eyes were opened to who she is as a person. You see Hailey was only focused on herself. She only did things that were beneficial to her. Grades, test scores, and homework among other things rewarded her for her efforts. She received the benefit of solid grades and a high grade point average, therefore she was rewarded for her hard work. She found it to be an abstract idea that she could also benefit by giving of herself in various ways through community service. It is this that changed her perspective of the concept. Community service is more than an ingredient on a college application; it can be a determining factor in deciding college acceptance between two similar candidates. Hailey learned through our conversations that community service shows a college who you are as a person. It shows what you value and what you're passionate about. Community service

> Community service shows a college who you are as a person. It shows what you value and what you're passionate about.

allows you to interact with others and help people in a manner that makes them happy. You know you are a responsible citizen by doing a nice task for someone, expecting nothing in return.

Hailey is in the midst of this journey. She is striving to find who she is outside of the classroom. The classroom is her security; community service is scary for her, not because she *can't* do it, but because it forces her to step out of her comfort zone. I have encouraged Hailey to do one thing each day that she is fearful of. Why? Because it will stretch her as a person. It will force her to step outside of herself to see that she is capable of achieving as much out of the classroom as she does within it. Community service challenges her to look at herself in the mirror and see beyond the surface to the core of who she is as a person.

I encourage you to do the same. Hailey is learning that community service is not about a stipulation for a college application. It is about her finding herself through what interests her. Community service should be a component of Hailey's life and a driving ambition for her to impact both her own life as well as the lives of those in need. Some become passionate about feeding the homeless, others become focused on Habitat for Humanity and building a home for those who don't have one. Hailey needed to find her passion for community service and discover that it will mean more to her than just a component of a college application. It's the journey that she is on, but she, like most students, will find out what drives her in due time.

After many months of thinking about it, talking with others including her parents, and considering her interests, Haley decided that her interest in school was where she could give back to her community. She decided to tutor other high school students after school through the National Honor Society. She chose this because she had a skill that could benefit others. As months went by she expanded her role beyond once a week tutoring to working with students on her own time outside of school four days a week.

Her senior year she expanded her tutoring role even further by going to the local elementary school after school and volunteering with students there. She worked with these little kids on their reading skills and comprehension. Before she graduated, Hailey shared with me that one of the teachers told her that she was able to improve some students' reading scores beyond the teacher's wildest expectations. Not only did Hailey help others through community service, but she learned the value of it as well.

By the way, she did *not* get admitted to the college of her choice. While she might have found this disappointing, her experience with community service made her see that this was just a bump in the road—not a black hole swallowing up her future. Hailey's response to the rejection: "It just wasn't meant to be . . . I can make a difference wherever I go!" And with that attitude—she certainly will!

SABRINA

Finding Your Career Path

I'm interested in seeing the different paths teenagers travel down as they go through their high school years. They are usually based on individual choices and are typically related in some way to one's personal interests. Sabrina was no exception. Sabrina was a student who aspired to attend a university after graduation. She had been thinking about some possible community service opportunities and was going to report back to me what she had decided.

She was a quiet, somewhat reserved student, but was extremely caring and empathetic toward others. A solid B+ student, she could excel in a wide variety of careers; it was just a matter of her deciding what career path to take. Sabrina had signed my clipboard letting me know she needed to talk to me. Next to her name she wrote the reason she needed to see me: to make a decision about community service.

Often, students seem upset when they come to my office, especially if they have made the request to see me, but Sabrina was just the opposite—full of smiles. "Sabrina you seem happy. What's up?" I inquired.

Excited, Sabrina responded, "I know what I want to do to give to those in need!"

"What did you decide?" I asked.

"Well, I was walking down the hallway and I walked by room 33. I watched the students in there for a moment and decided I wanted to work with them."

"That's fantastic—I'm sure they would want to interview you, but let me see if I can make it happen. I will call you down when I have an answer for you."

"Okay," Sabrina responded.

"Sabrina."

"Yeah?"

"I have to ask—Why them? Why that group of students?"

Sabrina explained: "You know, Mr. K, I have it pretty good. I am an only child, so I get what I want, and I have supportive parents. I was watching these students and I saw the challenges that they deal with every day. They struggle with things that I take for granted . . . the ability to walk, talk, eat, and communicate what they need.

It reminded me of how good I have it. If I could work with some or even one of these students to make their day a little easier then that would be amazing."

Sabrina left an imprint on me that day. I walk by those students all the time. For her to respond the way she did not only shows the person she is, but it allows her to use the compassion and empathy that she exhibits every day to a new group of students with special needs. My high school is one of two high schools in the county that runs a program for students with cognitive impairments. This program works with these students on a daily basis teaching them basic life skills.

After much discussion Sabrina was approved as a student aide to work in the program for students with cognitive impairments. She did this one hour a day her senior year. The impaired students befriended her and felt so important. She completed numerous activities with these students, but mostly she loved helping them read. For Sabina, the joy on their faces when they finished reading a book was priceless.

This service project had a profound effect on Sabrina's life and ended up altering her career plans. She had planned to study business in college, but her experience affected her so much that she decided to study special education. She was even awarded a full scholarship to attend the university that most interested her.

Sometimes giving to those in need has a unique way of affecting the giver. This is what happened to Sabrina, and it can happen to you. Look for a need and serve. In the end you will be amazed at how it changes you for the better, opens your eyes to the world around you, and causes you to appreciate what you have. We need more people willing to serve in this world. You can be the one to help bring about this change.

LINDSEY

Putting On a Show

Lindsey embraced serving her community. She was a solid, well-rounded student but, just like Hailey, she chose to take her personal interest and make it available to those elementary students who didn't have the same opportunity.

The passion that drove Lindsey was theater arts. She loved drama and played an integral part in the success of the high-school theater arts program. Lindsey loved every aspect of play production: from learning the dialogue, to the costumes, to building sets. She was a wonderful actress and she earned many of the plays' lead roles, but she loved to see all of the components of a play come together in an actual performance for an audience.

In an effort to give back to her community, Lindsey wanted to start an after-school theater program at a local library for elementary school students. She decided to invest in this project because she learned about theater primarily as a high school student; she wanted to expose the world of theater to a younger generation. She wanted kids to realize that there were other activities besides organized sports. Additionally, she felt that the arts were an area that always seemed to be lacking or the target of budget cuts. This was a way for her to "stand in the gap" and fill a need.

In order to make this idea a reality she met with officials at the community library, who were thrilled to learn of her plans. She promoted the idea at a couple of area elementary schools after meeting with the principal at each school. This resulted in information going home along with a registration form so students could sign up. She met with these kids on a regular basis helping them choose roles, learn their lines, and paint set designs and backdrops. The students would then perform their play for parents and other people who happened to be at the library that day. The students felt a sense of belonging. They had a place. They felt important. They were loved and valued.

Lindsey had about twenty kids volunteer for the program and, all things considered, everything went quite well. Almost five months passed from first talking to library personnel to a Saturday morning performance in April. Lindsey put a lot of smiles on the faces of both kids and parents and I am sure she felt a huge sense of personal satisfaction as well. That is what community service is all about. Community service is about giving back. It's about helping people in need and giving people a helping hand up instead of a handout.

> Community service is about giving back. It's about helping people in need and giving people a helping hand up instead of a handout.

Lindsey valued helping others. She saw a need and filled it instead of waiting for someone else to step up and fill the void. She took something that she was good at and used her abilities to help someone in need. The only person who can use your abilities is you. No one else can use them, so give back and serve. It doesn't matter whether you invest your time in a community theater arts program or dig wells in Africa. What matters is that you realize that regardless of where you are in life and what you have been through, you can always find someone who needs more help than you do. Lindsey

> The only person who can use your abilities is you.

found her niche in community service and in due time Hailey did as well.

Giving back allows us to see that there is good in this world despite the emphasis on the bad, and even teenagers can be a catalyst to bring about good. Performing community service shows you are observant of the needs around you and caring enough to *do* something about it. Community service allows teenagers to make a difference.

A real passion for community service comes from a genuine concern for others, and a belief that you can give them hope. There are needs in every community. I encourage you to seek out your local church, school, or community agency among others to find out what needs currently exist within your community, or check out resources online. Put a smile on someone's face and be in awe of how—like Hailey, Sabrina, and Lindsey—your smile grows a little bit bigger simply because you did something nice for someone.

POINTS TO PONDER...

✔ Do you believe community service is an indicator of who you are as a person? Why or why not?

✔ Community service is about helping people in need. Are you willing to give people a hand up instead of a handout? What is the difference?

✔ Why is it so difficult for some people to help those who are struggling through community service?

✔ You can always find someone who has gone through worse things than you. Never lose perspective of how far you have come.

✔ Performing community service shows a college you want to attend that you care about others. It allows them to see what you value and what you are passionate about.

✔ A passion for community service comes from being concerned by how someone is living and doing something about it. Is this you?

✔ Always appreciate what you have. Yes, you could always have more, but you could always have much less as well.

Chapter 5

PLANNING FOR COLLEGE

Before you know it, you will be walking across the stage at graduation to receive your high school diploma and you will embark on your college years. Trust me, you will be amazed at how fast your high school years pass by. You come from being a nervous freshman to a graduating senior in what seems like the blink of an eye. Within those high school years come tests, quizzes, and papers, as well as Friday night football games, homecoming dances, and prom. These events become more memorable when a student goes through his or her high school years while planning for college simultaneously.

College planning is a process that involves much thought, discussion, and

> College planning is a process that involves much thought, discussion, and maturity.

maturity. Planning for college involves not only making decisions, but making the *right* decisions. Planning for college is probably one of the things that I do most often behind the closed doors of my office. I take great joy in helping students with this process and sharing in the excitement of what will surely be a great and memorable time in their lives. My conversations with the kids are all different; like snowflakes and fingerprints, no two students are exactly the same. Each student has a different agenda, career path, and financial situation.

Some students might tell me they are not planning on attending college. I tell them to consider a vocational school. Learning a trade can catapult you into a successful career. Plumbers, mechanics, electricians, and heating/cooling specialists, just to name a few, use skills that can lead to rewarding careers. While you will most likely earn more in your career interest by attending college, you must find a career that you enjoy. Be passionate about your career pursuits. While financial security is important you must love what you do for a living. Unlike school, you will not have months off in the summer, and a schedule that changes each year. In the "real world" you will be doing the same job on a daily basis—so you'd better love it or you will be miserable!

Students are not all the same. You can't put everyone on a conveyor belt, on the same college path because high school seniors are not like cars; they do not roll off the assembly line one right after another with exactly the same specifications. They have different interests, different grades, and different career aspirations—*especially* those planning on going to college. Because of this I seek to tailor the college planning process to each student. Some students are self-motivated and seek to do much of planning for college on their own, while others seek my counsel on a daily basis. Here are some of their stories.

DEREK

Where Do I Go from Here?

Derek was one of those students who sought my advice on almost every aspect of his college planning process. I don't solve the problems of my students. I help my students solve their own problems. This is a better means to help them prepare themselves for life. Why? The reality is that you need to have the skills to work through your own problems. Sure, it's easy for you to ask a parent, but your parent won't always be around. If your car breaks down, how do you address that problem? You likely would call home. What if no one was there and you could not reach your parents? Would you just sit on the shoulder of the road until they called you back? No, you would be forced into action. You would have to come up with a solution to your problem. Working through your own struggles now allows you to learn how to face bigger obstacles in the future and deal with them appropriately. Derek was no exception, although he was in my office frequently; I hoped to help him find his own solutions.

> I don't solve the problems of my students. I help my students solve their own problems. This is a better means to help them prepare themselves for life.

One on particular day, Derek entered my office and was completely flustered. He sat down. His face was flushed and he seemed nervous or stressed. His legs were shaking as if he was on the edge of a panic attack. I closed the door, which was then followed by several minutes of silence. I could tell it was going to be an interesting conversation.

Derek came in with a crumpled paper on which he had a list of his preferred colleges. He had narrowed it down to four institutions, which apparently caused him much anguish.

"What's wrong, Derek?" I asked in an empathic tone.

Derek responded with a big sigh.

"Derek, did you complete and submit the applications online as we had discussed in past conversations?"

"I did back in October," Derek responded with relief.

"If you applied why do you seem so down?

Derek responded, "Because I got admitted—to all of them!!"

"Congratulations!" I declared with joy. "Isn't that a good thing?!"

"Yes, but I don't know which college to go to. Mr. K, how do you know what college you are supposed to attend?"

Derek had many things to think through. He was certain that he wanted a college education, but he never really considered what he wanted out of his education. I believe this to be the most important decision to make when selecting a college. You have to determine the level of investment you are willing to make in your college education. Do you want a diploma that shows you completed the necessary coursework, or do you want to absorb as much knowledge as possible and utilize it to catapult you into a successful career? This choice is critical because it is foundational to your education and ultimately what college you attend. The answer to this issue really is seen in your approach to academics at the end of middle school or, at the latest, the first semester of your freshman year.

Derek aspired to attend a more elite university. His approach to his academics allowed him to have multiple college options on the table. Getting a degree as opposed to getting a diploma is something that Derek and I talked about at length. I asked Derek:

> "What does your college education look like?"
>
> He responded, "What do you mean?"
>
> I asked, "What do you want out of it?
>
> "To learn?" Derek said with a confused look on his face.
>
> "What do you want the learning to look like, what do you want out of it?"
>
> Derek replied, "I don't understand."

Derek was certain he wanted to go to college and he insisted he was someone who aspired to greatness. I explained to Derek that there are failures, mistakes, and setbacks on the way to greatness. There is a learning curve to life. Mistakes are inevitable; how you respond to those mistakes is what will mark your education. The educational style one receives is critical. In Derek's circumstance did he want a lecture-oriented style of learning? Did he want one that consisted of working with other students through being part of an honors college? Would he like to have an internship as a part of his education? Did he want to network with other professionals in the field he is studying to give him some connections down the road for a possible future job or career? Was he interested in a study-abroad program, where you live in another country for a semester to continue your education? Finally, at what level of learning did he want to gain his knowledge and understanding? Derek had to determine whether he was someone who wanted to learn the information to get a degree—or was he someone who wanted to engage and interact with the knowledge?

There is a big difference in gaining a degree from a community college and a university, or a public university versus a private institution. There is also a big difference in gaining the same degree from an in-state college versus a university on the other side of the country. The decision of where to attend college shapes not only the depth of education one will receive, but the style in which it is delivered as well. You have to assess how the learning at the college of your choice is done. Does it include lecture, projects, group work, and internships or some other instructional methods? The learning style should be considered because the varied styles of delivery can increase the depth of the learning achieved.

Many students and their parents often look at location and most importantly, cost when considering what college to attend. I would never minimize the cost of college when considering where to attend. However, one must also consider the education and opportunities offered through studying at a given college or university. I will often ask my students to visit a university and talk to the college admissions department and ask: Why should I go here instead of another university? Ask that question to professors, faculty, and even current students. A key element in selecting a college is to determine what one school offers that another one does not; for example: internships, summer programs, study-abroad programs, networking opportunities with corporations, or job placement programs after graduation.

Derek left my office that day feeling overwhelmed. He had a lot to think about. For Derek, going to college was a guarantee. He had to decide what kind of college and educational experience he wanted, then consider such factors as cost, location, college size, and scholarship opportunities.

Selecting a college is so much more than a decision. It's the "on ramp" to the highway of life. College sets you on a path for your future. Attending college establishes who you are and what you aspire to become. College offers you education, knowledge, and understanding, but only if it is received, pondered, absorbed, and lived out by you.

> College offers you education, knowledge, and understanding, but only if it is received, pondered, absorbed, and lived out by you.

Additionally, there is nothing wrong with attending your second choice college. You can still reach all of your goals. Just because you can get accepted or admitted to a college with greater academic standards doesn't mean you should attend it. Attending a more elite school and having to struggle to stay there might not be as good for you as thriving at another college that fits your learning style and offers you a greater variety of opportunities.

ERIN

Choices, Choices, Choices

I had a student named Erin who had great aspirations of going to the University of Michigan. The University of Michigan is one of the premier public universities in the country and as a result has extremely rigorous admissions standards. She was very excited when she was accepted, and couldn't wait to be a Wolverine and enjoy all of the opportunities that go along with attending there—from great academics to the exhilaration of attending Michigan sporting events, campus activities, and organizations.

However, less than a year into her college experience, she began considering a transfer to a college closer to home. Although academically she was doing fine, she struggled with being away from home as she was close to her family. Erin had a hard time dealing with her frustrations about this, not understanding why she couldn't manage things better. After speaking with her when she'd come back to visit, I think she had in her mind what college would be like. She had dreamed of attending Michigan ever since she was a young girl, in part because her dad attended Michigan. Erin had certain expectations of college life, but she never considered that she might feel homesick. The university she considered transferring to back home was very well-respected and had initially offered her a full scholarship valued at more than $80,000. She turned down this scholarship to attend Michigan. If she were to transfer back, she would not be entitled to any of the scholarship dollars that she declined; this greatly bothered her.

After much conversation Erin decided to remain at Michigan. Her family visited her often and she became more involved in campus life. As the weeks went by she began to feel a sense of belonging, as if the University of Michigan was where she should be. The new friends she made went a long way in helping with that.

> Too many teenagers graduate from high school and flounder in college because they went to the wrong university and/or were directed to the wrong major.

Too many teenagers graduate from high school and flounder in college because they went to the wrong university and/or were directed to the wrong major by family, friends, or another adult. Some would say that Erin made a poor choice in a college even though she went to a prestigious university because she gave up tens of thousands of dollars in scholarship money. In the end things worked out for Erin. Everyone has opinions of what you should do. But everyone's factors in selecting a college are different as is each student's financial situation.

Select a college with realistic expectations of what the experience will be like. Don't let the social side of being at a college impair your judgment. Talk to those you trust, but in the end make the decision that's best for you. College is first about education; everything else is second. Choose one that fits your career interests and your personality.

Some see college as an obstacle because it is the door they walk through to life; others see it as the pathway to a successful future. Selecting a college may be scary, but with research, a college visit, asking the right questions, and knowing who you are and what you want, it can be a manageable process. The goal is college graduation with an education that propels you into a successful career. During college planning, don't constantly think of all that you need to finish before you get there; instead, pause for a moment and appreciate how far you have come in the process. Starting early in the college search process (partway into your junior year) will go a long way in helping you make the appropriate, thoughtful decisions.

> The goal is college graduation with an education that propels you into a successful career.

POINTS TO PONDER . . .

✔ College planning is a process. Take your time as it involves much research, discussion, thought, and maturity.

✔ You must determine the level of investment you will make in your college education. Do you want a diploma or do you want to learn as much as possible so it will catapult you into a successful career?

✔ There is nothing wrong with attending the college that was your second choice.

✔ Begin your college search sooner rather than later; there is no substitute for time and preparation.

✔ Make the college selection process your own. Don't let your friends dictate where you attend college and what you study. Follow your dreams and make them become reality.

✔ What kind of college experience do you want to have? Do you want to learn through lectures, group work, internships, study-abroad programs, or some combination of all of them?

✔ Look at college planning as the pathway to future career success and not as an overwhelming obstacle, filled with fear of making the wrong decision.

Part II
LIFE

Chapter 6

FAMILY

Your family is the driving force behind who you become. Typically, your parents and their values are ones that you adopt as you grow up and become what you value. You become a model of who your parents are. However, adults are not perfect and they can make extremely bad decisions that affect you—unless you consciously choose to avoid the poor choices they made.

> Your family is the driving force behind who you become.

In my office, I've witnessed both sides of the parenting pendulum. I've seen students who are being raised in healthy families enjoying the benefits that come with that. But all too often I've seen students struggle with all sorts of issues because their parents have trouble making wise choices.

Students have shared with me the family dynamics they deal with, many of which are complicated and out of their control.

Sometimes what's going on at home puts them in turmoil, causing them mental, physical, and emotional pain. This leads to them acting out in ways that only sabotage themselves and their future. Behind the closed doors of my office I have seen many students over the years express how they feel about their troubling family dynamics. Some students are frustrated and vent their anger at their parent's shortcomings, as the student perceives them. Others spend countless hours within a school year in my office in tears, desperately hoping that their situation at home will improve. Whether angry or sad, they all feel trapped because they have no control over what happens, or any way of making the situation improve—no matter how much they hope that it will.

For many students, their lives become a balancing act between taking care of their school work or academic issues, and striving to manage dynamics in the home as best they can. Some teenagers—whose parents have a chronic illness, or work more than one job to make ends meet, or have substance abuse issues—must play the role of parent themselves, even raising younger siblings. They struggle to manage school and these very adult responsibilities of cooking, cleaning, and helping siblings with their homework, prior to completing their own. Despite the difficulties, some appear to do well, while others struggle to manage their varied responsibilities and living situations.

Christmas break is far from comfortable or joyful for many students, and I find my office busier than usual prior to the vacation. It can be a time of high anxiety as students anticipate spending time with extended and immediate family members that they don't see on a regular basis. This often includes time spent with a parent they usually only see on weekends due to divorce. Additionally, these holiday events expose teenagers to family turmoil or drama, substance abuse issues, and so much more. Busier office hours also happen at the end of the school year, usually because these students know they have lost their counselor and the safety of their school routine as a source of coping and support over the extended summer vacation.

RACHEL

My Divorced Parents Live Together

One January, Christmas break had just ended and Rachel made a request to come see me. She wanted to update me on her family. I want my students to know that I am willing to listen if they want to share. This approach allows them to initiate the conversation. This permits them to see that sharing what's on your mind with a trusted adult can help relieve the burdens being carried. In Rachel's case, she was definitely willing to share.

Rachel lived in a home filled with constant fighting between her parents. They argued incessantly, even about trivial things that really didn't matter. Sometimes the fights turned into stony silence and the parents didn't talk for weeks on end. Rachel would go to school every day, hopeful that they would be talking when she got home, but when they did, the arguing, name-calling and finger-pointing would usually start the cycle anew. There was never peace and tranquility. I had met with her numerous times over the previous few years discussing how to cope with the conflict. When a person can't change a situation, learning coping mechanisms can be invaluable. One such skill is becoming resilient. This skill can help you navigate through life's inevitable turmoil.

After years of marital conflict, Rachel informed me, her parents had decided to get a divorce. This was tragic, but likely inevitable as the fighting continued. Rachel provided an update:

"How was Christmas?" I asked.

Rachel replied, "Christmas was great!"

I was glad to hear this, and I asked, "And how were your parents?"

Surprisingly, Rachel said, "Wonderful! To my surprise they got along very well."

"What changed? What happened to all of the fighting?" I asked, wondering what was different this time.

"They made some decisions about the two of them getting a divorce."

I asked, "What decisions did they make? Did they decide not to get a divorce?"

Rachel responded, "Oh, they decided to get a divorce; that has not changed!"

When I asked what had changed, Rachel said, "My parents have decided to live together in the same house even though they are going to get a divorce! How strange is that?"

Knowing this was not a good plan, and hardly a solution, I nevertheless tried to remain nonjudgmental, asking, "Interesting . . . what is that going to look like?"

Rachel said, "I guess the plan is for us to live in the same house together and all of us will have our own bedrooms."

"How do you feel about those family dynamics of living together in the same house?" I asked.

Hesitating for a minute, Rachel responded, "Well . . . it sure is different. I have never heard of something like this happening before. My parents can't stand to be in the same room with each other. I guess they decided to live together because neither of them have enough money to get their own place. The economy's been bad and they haven't found very good jobs. These next few months should be interesting."

A month passed and quickly turned into six months and soon thereafter a year. Rachel shared with me that the living arrangement was awkward, but she tried to make the most of a bizarre situation. She seldom knew whom she could trust and respect as the dysfunction between her parents often impeded the relationship she could have with them. The daily reality was still constant arguing and bickering as her parents blamed each other for their circumstances. Peace at home only existed in Rachel's dreams. While the situation was new for Rachel, I've discovered that her situation is not unique. I have had several students over the years in this position.

Rachel told me, "It got *really* strange with all of us living under the same roof when they both started to date and bring their dates over to the house. It just got too uncomfortable to be around my dad, his girlfriend, and my mom all at the same time."

Our society puts enough challenges on teenagers. Home should be a safe haven and a place to regroup and solve problems, but often it is not. Rachel's parents' decision to live disharmoniously under the same roof, but in different rooms, only compounded the issues Rachel had to deal with. These complex circumstances created instability in her life. She desperately wanted a stable home, and she thought that the new arrangement would stop the arguing but still retain the sense of familiarity of her parents being together. She harbored the hope, as kids often do, that maybe her parents would reconcile and live happily again, but the strange living situation only created more stress and uncertainty.

Being a product of an unstable and dysfunctional home often breeds future instability. For many students home turmoil impacts their ability to focus in school. This dysfunction often results in a lack of effort and becomes the justification for a student to settle for mediocrity—in school and in life.

Family is meant to be a source of strength and stability for children. Ideally, families propel kids toward success by providing a stable environment in which to learn and succeed until they grow up and create lives of their own. Students can overcome the breakdowns and still excel. They need to be passionate about expecting more of themselves and must want something better for their own lives. We live in a selfish world, where parents can put their own interests above that of their children. Teenagers must overcome these struggles to make it in the real world, not to minimize them as if they don't exist, but to learn to cope with their family dynamics in a manner that allows them to excel in other areas of their lives.

Coping is how you handle a situation. Some students journal, others draw or paint, still others exercise, and some spend more time with friends at their houses (even eating dinner with them regularly). I have even had some students move in with a friend for a month or so, as a way to cope in a positive way with a difficult family situation. If you don't find a way to cope that works for you, the family chaos can swallow you up.

GINA

What I Did to Graduate

Gina was a student who strived to press forward even as her circumstances held her back. She came to our school as a tenth-grader and, as do many students, arrived at my office with a story to tell. Hers was very complicated, and filled with numerous obstacles and setbacks. Only a few weeks into the school year, I noticed that her attendance had taken a nosedive; she was only coming to school a couple of times a week. Given the fact that she was a new student, I wanted to get to know her to assess the situation so I called her down to my office. She arrived and nervously closed the door. As I would later find out she was uncertain of what to expect. She never saw her counselor at her previous school so she initially thought that she was in trouble, but that was not the case at all.

"Hello, Gina, how are you adjusting to your new school?" I asked.

Gina replied, "Okay, I guess."

"Gina, I noticed that since you started here your attendance has been poor. Would you agree?"

"Yes," Gina responded in a very quiet voice.

"Why are you not coming to school each day?"

Gina shouted, "I am sick a lot and stressed out!"

"What is stressing you out?" I continued.

"Home." Gina stated with frustration.

"What's going on at home, Gina?"

"Well, I moved here because my parents divorced. My mom does not have much money so we live in low-income housing and even there we can barely make ends meet."

"What about Mom, does she work?" I calmly asked.

Gina responded, "She works, but her job does not pay very much. She does not have a car. She can't afford one, so she takes the bus to work. Mom comes home from work around six, but then she goes in her room and shuts the door. Mr. K, this happens almost every night. If we talk it is really surface: 'How are you? How was your day?' She is always so tired from work and trying to make ends meet—there isn't much of a relationship at all!"

"What about Dad?" I asked.

Gina replied: "My dad just got kicked out of his apartment because he could not pay his rent. He does not have a car, either, because it broke down. He can't fix it because he has no money. My older brother is now going to move in with me and my mom."

"Where is Dad going to live?"

Gina, flustered, said, "I have no idea . . . I think with a friend."

Gina had a great heart. If you saw her walking down the street, you would never know that anything was wrong in her world. She looked like your typical suburban teenage high school student, and she enjoyed all the typical things: music, movies, dance, etc. Behind closed doors, at home where she *should* feel safe and secure, she felt like the world was caving in. Her story was filled with despair and hopelessness. Gina wanted to do well. She wanted to persevere through high school and graduate, but the setbacks and obstacles in her world seemed almost insurmountable. She was overwhelmed, just trying to keep her head above water, as she dealt with tough issues—finances, lack of transportation, living in an area riddled with poverty and crime—that would stress an adult, let alone a fifteen-year-old sophomore.

Her family offered her little support, and there was constant conflict between the two sides. This only magnified Gina's struggles and complicated her life, causing her to put school on the back burner. Surviving each day took top priority.

In the end, Gina lived with a friend for a while to provide greater stability and have a more reliable means to get to school. To make up for the classes she failed and fulfill the requirements to graduate, she had to take credit recovery classes. This cost money, but she borrowed it from the mother of the friend she stayed with. She lived there for a few weeks doing her classwork and paying off the debt by doing projects around the house. She later moved back in with her mom when she was in a more stable place. All of them celebrated together as Gina earned the necessary credits to put on a cap and gown and walk across the stage at graduation. Many people that day saw a girl graduate; I saw a model of resiliency. She wanted to graduate and did what was necessary to make it happen.

MONICA

Managing a Dysfunctional Family

We talk a lot about the importance of planning for the future. But this can be very difficult for students to do when issues at home force them to focus on just today.

This was the case with Monica, who lived at home with her brother, who was in his early twenties, and both of her parents. She also had another brother who lived out of the house. Things weren't great in the home, but they were manageable. Her mom struggled with mental health issues, which led to impulsivity. As time passed Monica's dad could no longer manage these problems, and he informed his daughter that he and her mother would be getting a divorce. Monica struggled to stay grounded amid the turmoil. When the divorce was finalized, Monica ended up living with her dad. This was necessary because her mom refused to take her medication. With her mom's mental illness colliding with her role of being a parent, Monica made the difficult decision to step away from her mother and break off their relationship.

With the support of friends and other key adults Monica was able to survive the instability within her family and graduate from high school. A turning point was when Monica decided that she no longer wanted to see her mother. This understandably brought up all kinds of emotions. Monica persevered and decided to seek counseling to help her work through the anger, love, sympathy, embarrassment, and pity—all of the conflicting emotions she had surrounding her ill mother.

While she chose this positive route to help deal with her struggles, her older brother turned to drugs to cope with the family dysfunction. This eventually led to his tragic and untimely death. Today, Monica strives to make her life the best it can be, in his honor. Sadly, however, her other brother continues down a road filled with drug abuse.

The stability of a parental unit in a home is what creates security. When the security of a family becomes broken, the children are put into a tailspin. They go into survival mode.

The stability of a parental unit in a home is what creates security. When the security of a family becomes broken, the children are put into a tailspin. They go into survival mode. Some do this in a manner that is healthy, but unfortunately most do not. Instead, they meander through life, often on their own, hoping to do the right thing. Without guidance, temptation and immediate gratification gets the best of them and leads them to make bad choices that can lead to disastrous consequences.

We are educating many students who live in an unparented society. Numerous teenagers today are trying to navigate life on their
own. They try to survive the shortcom-
ings that exist in their homes and deal
with consequences of choices they did
not make. They do this while striving to

We are educating many
students who live in an
unparented society.

learn about relationships, deal with self-confidence, get an education, find out who they are, and plan for life after high school,
which hopefully includes college. Family drives success. Family
should act as guardrails that guide us and help us avoid danger as
we travel down the road of life. Family is supposed to allow you to
have space and move toward independence, while still providing
accountability. We don't come into the world fully formed and
knowing what to do; we need to learn these things from adults,
people with experience. The pressures and temptations of society
cause us to both need and value relationships. Family must be the
key component of these relationships, for that is who we spend the
most time with growing up.

Students who are fortunate enough to have stability in their
lives thrive, not just in high school, but in life, because they are
able to fully focus on their studies, and are given appropriate guidance in a safe and nurturing environment. There is no substitute
for significant parental involvement in the home.

Sadly, I've had students whose parents are not involved at all. I've
counseled students whose parents are in jail, who are homeless, live
in a hotel, have a home or an apartment but no electricity because
they couldn't afford the bill, and struggle each day for food. With
absentee parents, or parents who are so mired in their own issues
they can't care for their kids, these teenagers are at risk of becoming

sad statistics. The issue becomes, how can teenagers manage the struggles of home when they can't change their parents' choices?

Trying to answer this question often keeps me awake at night. Is there a way out? Too many students have struggles that are much bigger than they can manage. If this is you, I encourage you to focus on what you *can* control—your school work, which gives you a future. Planning for your future can give you the hope that will keep you going through the tough times created by your family problems, allowing you to not only see the light at the end of the tunnel, but to reach it.

Also, I encourage you to find someone else in need that you can help, whether great or small. Having someone appreciate your efforts gives you satisfaction and a sense of accomplishment. Focusing on giving to someone else can also take your mind off of your own family struggles, which can give some moments of peace in the midst of a chaotic storm at home. Remember, you are only able to control your response to what happens in life. Managing your circumstances with supportive people around you as you plan for a positive tomorrow may make your family's dysfunction just a little bit easier to deal with.

Whether the issues at home are big or small, students must learn to cope in order to survive. Some teenagers I work with blame themselves for the problem within their families. They so long for the family or their parents to be united that they work to try to create peace in the home, or try to intervene in an effort to get their parents to avoid a divorce, or try to get them back together despite a divorce being finalized. Your parents are adults. They make their own decisions and are responsible for the consequences that come with those decisions. I recognize that their decisions may impact you, but you cannot control what they do or say to each other. Teenagers who excel despite family dysfunction thrive because they admit a problem exists at home and are able (with the help of a counselor, teacher, or friend) to invest their time and energy in what they *can* control.

> Teenagers who excel despite family dysfunction thrive because they admit a problem exists at home and are able (with the help of a counselor, teacher, or friend) to invest their time and energy in what they *can* control.

Some students overcome complicated home lives by pouring themselves into friendships. They value the honest relationships that they can have with their peers because that's what they don't get at home. Others immerse themselves into sports. They work out and practice so they will play better on the field. They use the unity and friendships within the team to distract them from the issues and hardships at home. Another way to survive a chaotic home today is by planning for your tomorrow. Committing to your academics allows you to simultaneously plan for college and ultimately a life all your own. With life come struggles and setbacks. Manage your emotions, don't avoid them! If you are angry, express it in a healthy manner. If you need to cry, let it out. Deal with it appropriately with the help of a counselor or another adult you trust. Don't run from how you feel; your feelings are real and authentically what make you *you*. Learn from your family's poor habits so you are sure to steer away from their behaviors. See the conflict between your parents and realize that you don't want those behaviors in your future marriage and family. Live each day working hard to ensure that your life is full of honest, healthy, happy relationships that benefit you.

POINTS TO PONDER . . .

✔ You become a model of who your parents are, unless you make a conscious decision to work hard and avoid the poor choices they made.

✔ What mistakes have family members made that you can learn from? What would you do differently?

✔ Family should be the guardrails you bump into as you travel down the road of life. They provide accountability so you don't veer off course. Make sure you are that for your family one day.

✔ What motivates you to want something better for your life even when family lets you down?

✔ Any ability to cope with family turmoil is found in your willingness to admit what you can and cannot control. Remember, you are not responsible for the poor choices of your family.

✔ Why do people often repeat the same mistakes as their family members? Why don't they do the opposite when they know the consequences of poor choices are so great?

✔ What will you do to live a life of success instead of setback? What parameters (accountability) will you put in place to help ensure you have a greater chance of success?

Chapter 7

SOCIAL MEDIA AND FRIENDSHIPS

I walk down the hallways of a high school every day just like you do. Not a day goes by that I don't see teenagers with white lines coming out of their ears, or bumping into someone because they are looking down at their phones. In fact, you may be one of those students. We are a plugged-in society, your generation especially. Some students listen to music and block out the world around them. Others rarely look up from their phones because they are so busy texting or posting something online.

Every generation has memories of certain products they used when they were growing up. For today's teenagers, I believe that smart-phone technology and its byproduct, social media, will be that marker. Texting, posting, and tweeting—these are all avenues of social media that drive teenage interaction. It probably makes your parents crazy, and I'll bet they've asked you, "Doesn't anyone make a phone call or have a real conversation anymore? Why do you have to text all the time?" Everything teenagers do today is driven by technology and the latest social media craze. Chances are that if I mention one platform, it will be outdated by the time this book goes to print. Just as quickly, it seems that the nature of friendship and face-to-face interaction has been replaced by virtual friendships and cyber "likes" and "followers."

In the not-too-distant past, teenagers spent hours on the phone with their friends, usually talking about nothing in particular. Those days are long gone. Meeting face to face today is almost unexpected. Some would even consider it a disruption in a social-media driven culture. While the form of interaction has changed, the topics remain the same: dating, music, sports, entertainment, and school gossip.

Most people are mistaken about teenagers and their investment in technology. Teenagers are not focused on the technology for technology's sake. What they really desire is the communication. Teenagers enjoy the focused attention they get and the immediate responses that come from texting along with the privacy, since no one can intrude on their "conversations." The digital age has given teenagers another means to express themselves as they seek to develop independence from their parents. It is this aspect of social media that has redefined how teenagers look at friendships.

> Teenagers are not focused on the technology for technology's sake. What they really desire is the communication.

I have been amazed at how friendships have evolved over the years, and how relationships have changed as a result of technology. It seems to me that people have more acquaintances than friends. Why do you think this has happened? How has the importance of friendships been compromised in daily living today?

I have experienced this even in my own life. Our society continues to evolve based on the newest technology upgrades, the latest chat room, cell phone, website, or app. Social media has changed our expectations for what we are seeking from relationships. I think the problem with this is that people have expected, and for some even demanded, instant friendships. Facebook declares: "Will you be this person's friend?" We want instant communication—instant gratification. There is little investment in a relationship anymore. We exist for the quick interaction. We e-mail or text with an occasional face-to-face interaction. There is no depth to the relationships. Taking the time to get to know someone seems like a waste of time. The mentality seems to be that there are better things that we can do with our time. If we text, post, or "tweet" someone, we have gotten what we want out of them. We got our question answered. The conversation is done. The relationship is surface-based and seldom goes deeper, and that seems to be okay with both parties.

> We want instant communication—instant gratification. There is little investment in a relationship anymore. We exist for the quick interaction.

The only time this becomes a concern is when something happens and trust and honesty within a friendship become an issue. The roots of the friendship are not established; therefore, the friendship does not have a solid foundation based on trust and honesty in times of crisis.

At the heart of the matter, life is all about people. The only legacy we leave when our time on Earth is done is the investment we have made in the lives of those around us. Who have you connected with? Who is in *your* community?

Everyone wants to have friends. Adults desire to have friends, be accepted, and have a group that they can live life with. Teenagers desire the same thing. They long to enjoy the high school experience with other people. Friendships are what make high school more memorable. But teenagers often have multiple insecurities which lead them to question their self-worth, self-esteem, and have issues with trust and honesty. High school friendships can be a balancing act: you want to be accepted by your peers, but you also want to stay true to who you are and what you stand for and believe in.

Although most teenagers want healthy high school friendships, for many it's difficult to figure out where they fit into the high school social scene. Social media has become a means to express feelings. Brandon was a high school student who used social media to express his thoughts as he battled with being authentic with others about his life.

BRANDON

Posting a Cry for Help

Brandon was a sophomore who came from a divorced, dysfunctional home. He had been in my office several times before, but seldom spoke. He held everything in, but always seemed to have a lot on his mind. Though it seemed Brandon wanted to share what he was thinking and feeling, he never seemed able to express himself. I decided to watch Brandon closely because we'd had such limited conversation.

A day or two later another student saw one of Brandon's posts on a social media site and, concerned for his safety, she rightfully brought it to my attention. I always sensed he was a troubled student, but Brandon's post led me to intervene. It said:

> *I wear a mask called happiness. What it hides is all of the pain, hurt, anger, and rage inside of me. I act like an idiot to hide all of my emotions so I don't hurt my friends. I do this to defend my family and friends and shield all of my hurt from them. My life feels useless, like I have no reason to exist on this planet.*

Brandon's post was a cry for help. Social media gave him a voice where he felt he could safely express his thoughts and feelings. This expression of emotion was easier than talking to his parents or a trusted adult. Luckily a friend saw his post and intervened on his behalf, and we were able to get Brandon the counseling he needed before he did something dangerous and drastic.

I often tell people that going to counseling is like taking medicine when you have the flu. The prescription may taste terrible and make you cringe and want to spit it out. Counseling is the same in that it causes you to talk through a lot of your inner personal thoughts and feelings, those that maybe you have never shared with anyone before. This is not easy. It can be embarrassing and even scary, which is why most people just try to bury these feelings and avoid them. People who are struggling often keep things inside and try to present in person or online that they are fine, when on the inside they are in turmoil. Talking through your issues in counseling sessions allows you to gain a new perspective or new understanding about your problems and concerns. It can allow you to see things with greater clarity and understanding. Just as medicine relieves you of your flu symptoms, counseling allows you to feel better about yourself and the issues in your life.

It took Brandon months to work through his issues at a counseling center outside of school, but in the end his experience had a successful outcome. It was not easy, though. There were many bouts of anger, which at times turned into rage. At his most vulnerable moments he shared with me how he cried uncontrollably in his counseling sessions, but he got the help he needed. That does not happen to everyone. In this case social media was the avenue that was used to help someone in need. Sometimes online posts are a cry for help; however, many online posts become a way to harass and bully other students.

Too many times I have seen how social media is used to hurt others. Some teenagers bully others because they see it as a way to have some "fun" at someone else's expense. They rarely consider how hurtful it is to be on the receiving end. Bullying is designed to embarrass and humiliate others; social media makes it easier because it is fast, convenient, and often anonymous.

I have had students behind the closed doors of my office bring in pages and pages of online conversations full of hurtful comments. Students willingly give me their cell phones, which provide detail and evidence of the threats (usually through texting) that have been made against them. These circumstances are all too common.

While social media is a quick means of contact, it also allows for bullying and harassment to be carried out at any time day or night. What makes social media even more complex is that even if you don't see the negative postings about you, others see them. This has an impact on how other people treat you.

Social media serves a purpose. It allows for connection. It encourages you to seek out those whom you have lost contact with. It's a unique way to enhance friendships. But you need to be cautious: social media can also create division within a group of friends.

Cassidy, below, thought social media was strengthening her friendships, but she learned that her "friends" had other motives.

CASSIDY

You're Not Who I Thought You Were

Cassidy was a rather mature eleventh-grade student, but struggled socially. She desperately wanted to be friends with a particular group of fellow juniors in school. Cassidy did everything she could to be part of their inner circle. She went out to lunch with them and they attended late-night movies together on the weekends. Sometimes they would hang out for hours together, just talking, and even when they were not together they would text each other all the time, often well past midnight. Any onlooker would have concluded that they were the best of friends.

Cassidy wanted to be the friend who always knew what was going on—to have the "inside scoop." She thrived on gossip. Because of this, Cassidy would often get tangled in a web of drama. This time the drama was about her friends, which would ultimately lead to the truth about their relationship.

The truth was that they were using her for her car and her ability to drive whenever they went out. Although some of them had their licenses, none of them had their own car or access to one on a regular basis. They befriended Cassidy, but in their eyes she was on the outside of the group. They just wanted transportation whenever they wanted to go out.

As the school year went on, they began texting one another and talking online about how much they did not care for Cassidy. Once, when they were all eating lunch at a local fast food restaurant, she overheard them talking badly about her as she came back to the table from the bathroom. Cassidy was shocked, completely crushed, and humiliated.

Later, she saw what her "friends" had posted online—mean, hateful, degrading comments that were not true. She had been completely unaware that this had been happening. Social media allowed her peers to mock her to their vast online networks. It was easy for them and they didn't have to see the damage that their viciousness had done to Cassidy.

One of the things that Cassidy had such a problem with was that these weren't anonymous individuals—she considered these people her friends. They had spent so much time together and she had shared a lot of personal things with them about her life. She trusted them and confided in them. She felt so naïve and betrayed.

Even after all of this she still wanted to be friends with these people. She thought that maybe if she changed some aspect about herself, she could fix whatever was wrong and make them realize what a good friend she was. She texted all of them in the hope that she could convince them that she was a valuable friend to them, worth more than just her car. Unfortunately, they did not see her value, and the interaction through texting did not go well. Conversations, as well as arguments, are usually not successful through texting, e-mails, and social media. Face to face or, in the absence of that, telephone conversations are still best when discussing important issues. It might be more frightening, but you need to be honest and be yourself. You don't have to prove to others that you are a nice person if you and those closest to you believe you are kind and sincere. Sometimes, instead of trying to repair a friendship, it may be better to let them go, as difficult as it may be. Cassidy had to learn this.

Cassidy ended up losing basically her entire network of so-called "friends." She became depressed and struggled academically. Cassidy's mother put her in counseling for several months, which allowed her a safe place to work through her emotions. Through counseling Cassidy realized she needed to give up trying to create friendships with these people. She had reached a place where she accepted that she couldn't force authentic friendships to happen. Afterward, Cassidy had a new outlook on life—and she will never look at texting and social media in the same way.

While some teenagers use social media to harm people, others use it in a manner that inadvertently puts themselves in embarrassing situations. Some online posts are done as a means to generate attention, which can lead you down a dangerous, chaotic road. These are sometimes sexual in nature and usually involve girls taking inappropriate pictures of themselves and sending them to their boyfriend or posting them online. I wish I could say this was rare, but I have dealt with this many times, and have seen the disastrous outcome. You probably can think of someone who did this. Maybe you have done this. Teenagers who do this come from all walks of life; what they have in common is wanting to be noticed or valued.

What might start as an inappropriate picture sent to a boyfriend —one person—can quickly mutate into a viral post that spreads like wildfire. The boyfriend forwards it to his friends and those friends forward it to others or post the photo online. Before you know it, hundreds of students end up with the picture of the teenage girl.

Reading this, you are probably not surprised that this would happen. Most would expect that teenagers would forward a photo like this to their peers. While social media can be a great tool, there really are no boundaries with it in the hands of most people, especially teenagers. Everything seems to be fair game. It is this mentality that brings about further consequences for all involved.

Depending on the state you live in, there is a strong possibility that the hypothetical students in this scenario would face criminal charges for distributing child pornography. Most of these laws were on the books before smart-phone technology, and are aimed at adults. A student eighteen or older is considered an adult and can find him- or herself in deep trouble that can ruin their future in the blink of an eye. A maximum penalty for such an offense can be *years* in jail under mandatory sentencing laws, and can require a student to register as a sex offender for the rest of his life. In some cases, this can apply to teenagers who engage in this activity who are under eighteen. This punishment can significantly impact a student, not just in high school, but forever. What do you think a college admissions office would think when they see this on a student's record? Finding a job would be equally difficult, as would finding a place to live since there are restricitons on where sex offenders can live.

The crime committed here does not deserve suspensions and criminal charges; instead, those involved need counseling. A ten-day suspension for an offense such as this achieves nothing. When you are using social media, you always need to be aware, and think before you click "send" or hit "post." What images are appropriate? What language is appropriate? What do you choose to do and say in social media? Something immature that you post today could, realistically, hurt your chances for a job down the road. What you type and post online can stay there for many years, even decades.

Likewise, if you see something that is unnecessary or inappropriate, will you let it go or will you speak up? Social media provides opportunities for communication, but along the way it is plagued with subtle traps of temptation that can lead to despair, embarrassment, and consequences. My office fills on a regular basis with students who are having friendship issues. Social media plays a role in many of them. Almost all of these issues are among girls, in large part because of the roundabout nature of their interactions. For instance, if Julie has an issue with Kari she doesn't go and tell Kari, she asks Stephanie what she thinks. Stephanie then isn't sure what to do so she asks Kaley and so on. When more people are involved, the conflict naturally escalates, as does the chance that friendships will be fractured. Amanda learned this all too well.

> When more people are involved, the conflict naturally escalates, as does the chance that friendships will be fractured.

AMANDA

What Does a "Real" Friend Look Like?

Amanda was a sophomore. She was one of those teenagers who was a true friend. She was loyal, honest, and trustworthy. It all sounds great, but she was having issues with her peers. She wanted to see me so I called her out of Spanish class. When she arrived in my office she seemed agitated. After some conversation, I said:

"Amanda, what brings you in today, what's going on?"

She couldn't seem to sit still, and kept shifting back and forth in her chair. "Friends!" she told me.

"What about them?" I responded.

Amanda grew more restless, got up, and started pacing back and forth. "I need to know how you know a friendship is real. How do you know you have a true friend? With social media it seems everyone knows everything. It's hard to trust people . . . so how do you know a friend is *really* your friend? How do you know?!" She sounded nervous and frustrated.

Amanda was friends with all different groups of people. She questioned herself because she was unsure of *who* she was, in that she tried to be a different person depending on who she was hanging out with. She drank to fit in at parties to be friends with those who partied. She worked hard in school so she could be friends with those who wanted to succeed in school. She even slept with guys so she could be friends with that group and gain their acceptance. She had relationships with all of these people in person and online. The true issue was that Amanda was not in conflict with her friends, she was in conflict with herself. She had no idea who she was and what she wanted in a friend because she was too busy constantly changing to please the "friends" she was with at a given time.

> When you are true to who you are, then you can be a true friend.

Amanda began to see through our conversations that when you are true to who you are, then you can be a true friend. You remain authentic to your morals, values, and convictions and you don't waver from them just to be accepted by a person or group. Too often teenagers (especially girls) strive for acceptance at the expense of self. A key element in personal disappointment is trying to please everyone. The challenge for Amanda was to find a balance between giving in a relationship and getting something from the relationship. Amanda worked through these issues over a few months and began to see areas in her life where she needed to improve.

Amanda's eyes were opened to who she was around her peers and the changes that she had to make for her own well-being, and for the authentic friendships that she wanted to develop with others.

Over the next two years, Amanda ended friendships as well as dating relationships in an effort to help her find herself and what she really wanted in a friend. Quality friendships remain a journey for her even two years later as she struggles to trust people to determine if their actions are sincere. But now she knows both who she is and what she wants in people. Amanda realized that she has to be honest with herself and look at a relationship for what it is and not what she wants it to be like.

Cameron could have helped Amanda deal with so-called "friends" since he was able to handle peer pressure so well.

CAMERON

Why I Left the Party

Cameron was a solid student whom I had known his entire high school career, although I really was able to get to know him during his junior year. He was one of those students who was mature and grounded. He came from a solid family and seemed to have a real sense of how to manage relationships even when he was pressured to conform to those around him. Cameron was well-liked within his circle of friends, but was not someone that I would consider "popular," meaning someone who is accepted by a wide variety of social groups within a school regardless of his own interests. This was not Cameron because he was *known* by others, but not *accepted* by them. He was a balanced person both academically and socially.

He showed up at my office one day without warning.

"How was your weekend?" I asked.

"Unexpected," Cameron stated.

"What does that mean? What did you do?" I inquired.

Cameron shared, "I went to a party over the weekend that I was invited to."

"How was the party?" I inquired.

"Interesting!" he responded.

"Really? How so?"

"I was pressured to smoke marijuana!"

"What did you do?" I said.

"I didn't do it! I said I didn't want to."

"Good for you!" I said proudly.

"Thanks," Cameron said. "They also asked me to drink, but I left."

"Great, but why did you leave?"

Cameron said: "I left because I knew that if I left I wasn't going to miss anything!"

What an amazing response to peer pressure! Wanting to go along with the rest of the crowd in order to "fit in" is a subject that teenagers face on a regular basis. Your parents faced it. I faced it. Everyone faces it at some point, boys and girls. Drugs, alcohol, smoking, and sex are usually the most common forms of peer pressure faced by teenagers today. The stress is constant and is evident online, through texting and tweets, and certainly through conversation and gossip.

Cameron was invited to a party hosted by his friends, or so he thought. These were people he knew and that he thought he could trust. Cameron and I spoke at length in my office that day about friends and the pressures that can come with those friendships. Cameron was very honest with me, sharing that his friends are there to help him be a better person because he is trying to do the same for them. If they are unable to do that, he said, then he does not want them in his life.

It's easier to avoid peer pressure when friendships are seen as a bonus—not a requirement for you to survive. Friendships require honesty. Peer pressure is often subtle. It usually occurs when you don't expect it and often when many people are around.

> It's easier to avoid peer pressure when friendships are seen as a bonus—not a requirement for you to survive.

Cameron was able to avoid peer pressure because he stayed true to himself and what he believed in. His beliefs and values allowed him to filter difficult situations. Peer pressure is never positive, if it was it would not be considered pressure. It would be encouragement, support, or something similar so as to promote something positive. Friendships make life more enjoyable, but one poor choice because of peer pressure can lead to a lifetime of consequences.

> Peer pressure is never positive, if it was it would not be considered pressure. It would be encouragement, support, or something similar so as to promote something positive.

Friendships are those pieces of life that should make us better people. They enhance life as an extension of your own family. In dysfunctional families, good friends can even become your family of choice. Social media can hinder the quality of the friendships you have because your individual friendship with someone becomes known by everyone. Life is about balance, and friendships play a big role in that balance. Those you may think are your friends but are not will use you, take advantage of you, and manipulate you to improve their own social standing even if it hurts how people look at you. Be cautious of your friends and make sure that they are an asset to your life. Can you trust them? Can you confide in them? Will they help you when you are struggling, or only when things are going well?

Social media gives teenagers a voice. This is a good thing because in the right situations it allows you to express yourself and your individuality. Social media lets others into your world and allows them to see and hear your viewpoints and values. It allows people to see who you are; however, the peer pressure to post pictures and comments online can alter how others perceive you so be careful what actions you carry out on social media. Additionally, I believe that many teenagers (adults as well) say and post things that they would *never* say face to face with someone. The truth is that online postings have consequences, and they can follow you for a lifetime. They can even (in some instances) lead to a criminal record and impact your high school graduation, admission to college, and your career. Be cautious about what you choose to post and do not let peer pressure influence your decisions. Recognize that social media may be fun, but it is full of pitfalls and traps that can sidetrack you from achieving greatness in your life.

Technology can let the world into your friendships, so be careful. You don't have to reveal all of the details of your life with every friend. Each friendship is different, special, and unique, just as you are. You will trust each friend to a different degree. This is not a bad thing; it shows that you know your friends and can appreciate their individuality. Take the time to know who your friends are

> The truth is that online postings have consequences, and they can follow you for a lifetime.

as individuals. This will go a long way in helping you avoid pressure situations as you will have peers who will look out for your best interests. Don't use social media as a substitute for spending quality time with your friends. Quality friendships will help you achieve the greatness that you are so capable of reaching.

POINTS TO PONDER...

✔ Friendships in high school are a fine balance between being accepted by your peers and staying true to who you are and what you stand for and believe in. How do you achieve this?

✔ Why do you need to be careful with social media? What are some of the problems that can arise from social media? Are there any changes you need to make to your own use of social media? How have your friends been affected by it, both good and bad?

✔ When our life is over, our legacy is the life we lived with the people around us. What is the legacy of your life as of today?

✔ Who are the three most meaningful friendships in your life and what makes them so special?

✔ Do you present yourself on social media the same way as you do when you are face to face with someone?

✔ Peer pressure is never positive, if it was, it would not be considered pressure. How do you choose your friends, and what do you do to manage situations filled with peer pressure?

Chapter 8

DIVERSITY

Our country is built on diversity. We are a population of varying races, ethnicities, ages, socioeconomic levels, religious beliefs, and more. Most of us usually go through our day and never consider the variety within the population around us. Living in a diverse population creates a need for tolerance, acceptance, and respect of differences. Diversity is striving to both recognize and understand the differences between people and to find value in those differences. This understanding builds bridges between people.

> Diversity is striving to both recognize and understand the differences between people and to find value in those differences.

I have seen diversity in high school just as you may have. Every day I see students of different races, ethnicities, and economic backgrounds walking the hallways. I see students plugged into their smart phones, yet I have also seen students with ear buds plugged into nothing but a block of wood or deck of cards because they can't afford a phone. All teenagers, regardless of their circumstances, seek to be accepted, and some will go to great lengths to fit in.

There is also diversity in terms of social status in high school. Although some students overlap categories, there can be divisions such as the athlete, band member, National Honor Society member, chess club participant, and cheerleader. In a misguided attempt to both be part of a group and also stay at the top of the social scene, too many teenagers look to expose weak points in their peers. These target areas may be appearance, race, poverty, athletic ability, or academic success. Because some students are more mature than others, the level of impact on each teenager varies.

Diversity allows us to learn from people from different backgrounds and circumstances. Being aware of the similarities and differences between you and other people can help generate an appreciation for what you have and your freedom as an American. However, for some it makes them feel worse and even resentful because it reminds them of the things that they don't have or can't afford. This feeling, if channeled properly, can be used as motivation to work hard and overcome these obstacles. This can inspire you to pursue and achieve more because of the opportunities that you have here in America.

Americans take so many of our freedoms for granted. These freedoms lead to the opportunities that so many from other countries long for. I am reminded of this when I deal with students who have moved here from overseas. The diversity issues that I deal with behind closed doors speak to the struggles and challenges that these students have to cope with and try to overcome. The differences truly lie in the stories that brought them to America.

Everyone has a different story to tell about who they are and where they came from. If we were all the same, life would be generic, dull, and our interactions boring. By learning to understand those who are different from us, we can grow beyond our own boundaries, become more well-rounded, and even gain valuable lessons from others' life experiences.

> By learning to understand those who are different from us, we can grow beyond our own boundaries, become more well-rounded, and even gain valuable lessons from others' life experiences.

OLA

America: Land of Opportunity

In a high school with such a diverse student population, I interact with students from all kinds of backgrounds. This allows me to see and really appreciate where kids come from, and what both they and their parents have had to face.

When Ola was four years old, she came to the United States with her mother and older sister from Albania, for more opportunity, especially the dream of going to college. Her father stayed in Albania while he sought to secure the necessary paperwork to join his family in America. Even at that age, it was a difficult transition for Ola, which she wrote about in the following college entrance essay. This experience played a role in her valuing education and shaping her future dreams. She wrote:

Apprehensively, I teetered into my new kindergarten classroom. The teacher and children spoke in a language foreign to me. They stared.

They laughed. After a week of unremitting silence, I was directed to the principal's office. My mother was there too, seated adjacent to the translator. The principal spoke and the translator began speaking.

"She says Ola needs special attention. She barely socializes with other kids and she's not learning anything."

My mother looked at me. She had newly developed circles beneath her eyes. I looked at the clock. It was one o'clock—at this time a month ago she would be coming home for her lunch break from her career as a clerk for a financial consultant in Albania. However, we had left that life, and started a new one. My mother now worked eighteen-hour days as a dishwasher in a restaurant. Our minimal condominium had been replaced by a grimy, musty one-bedroom apartment.

The translator said, "She suggests that Ola be placed into the English Language Learners (ELL) program to receive the extra assistance she needs."

My mother rose. "I will speak with my daughter, and I will call you with our decision."

Although she had been reduced to a mere dishwasher, my mother still spoke with her distinctive, authoritative voice.

Hand in hand, we marched out to the front of the school. Even her hands had changed; although they had always been hard-wearing and resilient, America had molded them into callous machinery that never seemed to stop working.

"Ola, do you know why Mommy brought you here to America?"

I shook my head. I could not grasp why my mother had traded our comfortable lives for new ones with seemingly endless obstacles.

"When I was younger, I had big hopes, big ambitions, and big dreams. I wanted to be someone. I wanted to change the world. As I grew older, in a culture in which women are subordinated and oppressed, those dreams were destroyed. I was told what role I would play in society's

theater. I had no voice, no power. I've lived a comfortable life; I haven't lived a fulfilled life.

"Your teachers think you belong in a slower-paced class because of your English skills. I'll let you decide. Think carefully, because every opportunity missed is an opportunity lost."

I have the utmost respect for students and families who transition from their homeland to America. They come here for opportunity, for a better chance at making their dreams become reality. However, this is not without difficulties. They have to learn a new language and culture, are often the victims of discrimination, and typically have to take menial jobs to make ends meet at least to start, even though they might have a university degree and may have held a professional-level job in their country of origin. The job transition adds an extra layer of stress as they go through the adjustment process, striving to learn an entirely new way of living.

Ola saw through the eyes of her mother that her life is in her own hands and she can make it whatever she chooses. She now has the opportunity to use her voice to change the world.

People often use diversity as a scare tactic, implying that those who are different will drain our resources, expect handouts, and maybe even make our communities less safe. This couldn't be further from the truth. Students like Ola demonstrate that diversity does not erode our society; instead, she paints a picture of those who value opportunity. Sure, there are obstacles along the way; there are obstacles for all of us. The opportunities America offers are why so many are willing to face these obstacles.

Like Ola, some teenagers (whom you will also read about in future chapters) have embraced the transition in coming to

America; however, for many others the move is slow, challenging, and oftentimes overwhelming. This is the way it was for Demetrius.

DEMETRIUS

Rockets Kept Me from Going to School

Demetrius was new to our school, having moved to the U.S. from Lebanon. His parents came for opportunity, as most do. He was really struggling in his classes. I saw Demetrius in the hallway before he went to gym class. He was walking alone with his head down. He wasn't carrying any textbooks or folders; this was common for him as he often showed up for class unprepared.

My goal in bringing him to my office was not to talk about his grades; it was to see if I could gain an understanding of his past. I wanted to find out his whole story, because I was certain there was more to it than struggling with typical academic issues.

He sat down in my office and I closed the door.

"How are you doing?" I asked.

"Okay, I guess," he said, hesitating.

"Demetrius, I was looking at your grades and I noticed you were struggling and, really, you have since middle school. So tell me about yourself. Where were you born?"

"I was born in Lebanon. My parents came over here for better opportunities to provide for the family."

I asked, "When did you move here to America?"

Demetrius responded, "I'm not sure, but it was about the end of elementary school."

"I see. Did you go to school in Lebanon?"

"Yeah, for a little while when I was really young."

This caused me to pause, but I continued, ". . . So you stopped? Why did you stop going?"

He explained, "I stopped going because of all of the shooting, bombs, and rockets."

"Was this for very long? Did this happen most of the day?"

"A long time—years! Sometimes it was all day and other times it was less."

Compassionately, I said, "I can't imagine what that must have been like."

Demetrius responded, "Many of my friends seldom went to school because our parents were always afraid we would get shot on the way there and die in the street. My mom could not handle the thought of me dying in front of our house so I stayed home. That is why I don't like the Fourth of July; all of the fireworks just remind me of war back home!"

Talking with students and entering their world through the stories they share humbles me. It makes me empathic to their circumstances, and shows the challenges that teenagers like Demetrius have to overcome. While I will never fully comprehend what living in a war zone is like, especially for a child, hearing Demetrius's story and listening to the hurt and pain in his voice showed me how much of an impact the war had on him, even after he left. People sometimes have deep wounds that are not visible to others. These are often the most difficult to heal because they are emotional. Demetrius's story also showed me how easy it is to take for granted the relative safety and freedom that we have in this country.

Demetrius demonstrated the many challenges that must be overcome by foreign students. His family came to America for safety and educational opportunity. But, because he stopped going to school in his home country, he lacked the essential skills needed to excel in the classroom in this country. Demetrius did graduate on time, through hard work on his part and daily tutoring support.

Respecting the diversity among my students has helped me appreciate their backgrounds and the stories that have shaped who they are today as teenagers. Remember, everyone has events in life that define who they are. They may be good, bad, or even tragic. Behind every story or event is a person. Take the time to walk in someone else's shoes by learning about their culture. You don't have to agree with everything someone stands for, but you do need to respect them. Differences between you and someone else are not wrong, they're just different. I learned this from Ursula.

> Take the time to walk in someone else's shoes by learning about their culture and its values. You don't have to agree with everything someone stands for, but you do need to respect them.

URSULA

Respecting Heritage versus Embracing America

Ursula was a senior. She was very social and excelled in the classroom. She loved to interact with people and get to know them. She moved to the United States from the Middle East when she was in preschool. She transitioned very well to the culture in America, but her parents continued to live in a manner consistent with the culture of their homeland. This made things difficult for Ursula because although she was not born in America, she felt as if she was. She has no recollection of her country of origin, since her family moved to the United States before she started kindergarten. This is a frequent challenge among students who move to the United States when they are very young.

The conflict with her parents was getting worse, as I learned with each passing visit to my office. Ursula stopped by again to update me on how things were going at home.

"So, Ursula, how are things?" I asked.

"The same," Ursula responded.

"Help me out, what does 'the same' mean?"

"It means that nothing has changed," Ursula said.

"What are you and your parents arguing about?" I asked.

"Two things. The first is we are arguing about them not letting me go away to college."

"Why is this an issue for them?"

"The cultural background of my parents holds to the idea or value that you are loyal to the family. They think the children should be so loyal that they would never leave home because it would make the family look bad. They are all for me going to college, but they want me to live at home so I can honor the family and my culture."

"Interesting . . . and how do you feel about that?"

"I want to go away to school. I want to challenge myself. I love my family, but I want to see what I am capable of achieving. A university away from home allows me to do that," she said, with a mix of determination and frustration in her voice.

I continued, "What's the other issue you are struggling with?"

"Dating!" Ursula proclaimed. "I want to date who I like or who I think is cute. My parents, and our culture, believe in arranged marriages—where your parents pick who you will date and eventually marry."

"Obviously, you disagree with this?"

Ursula responded, "Yes, I do! I want to date who I am attracted to! Who I like! It just seems weird to have my parents pick someone for me to love. It's kind of gross! I am not trying to disrespect my heritage. I have grown up my whole life in America so I see things a little differently because my experiences have been different from my parents. I never lived in the Middle East."

I have had many students who struggle with respect toward their cultural heritage. It becomes a real battle for a lot of teenagers. They really want to live their own lives, but they also don't want to be disloyal to their parents and their cultural values. Some can feel trapped. They can be torn because of the love and appreciation they have for their parents. They are thankful that their parents brought them to America for a better life, but they want to be able to make their own decisions.

Cultural diversity can pose challenges to these kids as they go through life. It may have been a challenge for you personally. I have really been able to see firsthand how gut-wrenching these issues can be. Every student's circumstance is different and I have had the privilege of learning from each one of them.

I counseled Ursula through the rest of her senior year. We discussed her going away to college versus attending a school in town and living at home. I told her that if she did go to school close to home, she'd still be away from home quite often. Many college students living at home end up primarily just sleeping there. Most of their waking hours are spent in class or studying at the library on campus.

Ursula's parents eventually agreed to let her go away to college provided that she would come home and visit on weekends every once in a while. While I never spoke with them, I had Ursula convey information to them. This aided their discussions as a family and led to them working through their differences. While they changed their minds on the issue of going away to college, they held fast to their view on Ursula dating; they would not allow her to go out with whoever she pleased. Unbeknownst to them and me, Ursula had a boyfriend—someone she had been seeing in high school for three years but concealed from her parents.

Finding a level of comfort between the demands of your parents based on culture and your own desires to date is not easy. I encourage you to value your cultural roots. As you grow older and become an adult it may become easier for you to make your own decisions, which your parents may be more willing to accept. Additionally, I encourage you to seek advice from a trusted adult as he or she may be able to help you navigate the various emotions that arise when dealing with such a difficult issue.

Another form of diversity is financial in nature. Money separates people and impacts all people regardless of culture or ethnic background. I frequently work with teenagers who have had great financial strain in their families. One student I worked with did his homework by candlelight because his parents hadn't paid the power bill and the company shut off their electricity. I've helped families get resources because they were scrambling to have food to eat. I have had numerous students and their families living in hotels and homeless shelters for all kinds of reasons. Some sought a shelter because of the loss of a job, still others because of domestic abuse, and others because their house burned down.

These students often feel that they can't achieve or be successful because of their social status. It's as though they give up before they even get started in life. They think that success is for other people, ones who live in nice homes and with two parents. They see their own poverty or broken home as an insurmountable barrier. They feel that because of their environment, the situation they are in, that they don't deserve anything good and can never expect success. This may be you or someone you know.

The truth is, you have the opportunity to be successful regardless of your environment and social status. You can achieve whatever you set out to accomplish. You can run through your barriers in life to make your dreams into reality. It may be difficult, but it is possible. If you want to achieve in life you *can* overcome your disadvantages. You can turn your trials into triumphs. You may have a higher mountain to climb to success and achievement than some of your peers, but you *can* reach the summit. Many teenagers would rather complain about their struggles and find excuses for why they fall short instead of doing something to bring about change. Be a difference-maker in your own life. Overcome your social status and diversity challenges. Be courageous. Let your story of resiliency inspire someone else. You may not be able to choose your parents, or the circumstances in which you were raised, but you can, through hard work and determination, set a successful course for *your* future.

> You may not be able to choose your parents, or the circumstances in which you were raised, but you can, through hard work and determination, set a successful course for *your* future.

Too many times we shun people who are in need. Teenagers and adults both do this, we run from people who are different from us for fear of feeling awkward or embarrassed. Circumstances change our experiences, but we are all people who should be both validated and valued regardless of our diversity. I believe we are better together. The more we help one another the more we all benefit. The more we appreciate our differences the more we truly can improve the quality of who we are as people which only makes our neighborhoods and communities better.

> I believe we are better together.

The diversity within your city, school, and neighborhood is what is unique to you. It defines your background and can enhance who you are as a person. Every one of us interacts with people of various races, cultures, and economic backgrounds, to name a few. We all have opportunities to learn from one another. The experiences I have had with my diverse population of students over the years have opened my eyes to the wonderful variety of people that I can learn from. There is great value in respecting cultural differences. If you can appreciate those differences, it will benefit you and the community in which you live for years to come.

POINTS TO PONDER . . .

✔ How can being aware of other people's differences help you to be more open-minded?

✔ What are some examples of diversity at your school?

✔ Do you appreciate the differences between people and get to know different people, or do you tend to avoid those who are different from you?

✔ What challenges did you have to overcome as a result of diversity? Did you have success in overcoming the challenge? Did it make you stronger?

✔ Why is "different" seen by many people to be "wrong," when it's just "different"? What does this mean?

✔ If we are supposed to be accepting of the differences among people, why is it so hard to do? How can you improve this in your own life?

Chapter 9

GRIEF AND LOSS

Nothing in life stays the same for long. Our ability to adapt to change is critical to our health and well-being. Losing a loved one, whether it is a family member or a friend, is part of the life cycle and we will all experience this many times at some point or another. The circumstance of that loss is what contributes to how a student may deal with the passing of someone they care about.

One of the things I love about my job, beyond working with teenagers and helping them plan for their future, is the fact that no two days are alike. Every day there is a different student with a different issue. What makes grief and loss so difficult is that those issues arise without warning. The grief that teenagers feel over the passing of a student varies. Every

> Every student deals with grief and loss differently, and every response is appropriate (as long as it is done safely) because each student processes their emotions differently.

113

student deals with grief and loss differently, and every response is appropriate (as long as it is done safely) because each student processes their emotions differently. I have had students cry, become angry, or retreat into silence.

MEGAN

Why Did This Have to Happen?

Grief is the process of responding to a life-changing loss.

Grief is the process of responding to a life-changing loss. Grief is a journey you go on when you lose a loved one. Behind closed doors, students come to me with a variety of emotions over a loss. I help them try to process their feelings in a safe environment. Oftentimes, it is the circumstances around the loss that dictate the ease with which the student proceeds and processes it. Megan was a student who suffered such a situation. I happened to be out in the hallway one day, and found her in tears. She came into my office. I closed the door as Megan struggled to keep her emotions in check.

Megan had just learned that her former boyfriend, who moved to Texas a year earlier, was killed in a construction accident where he worked. Although they had broken up, they had remained close friends. I knew Megan very well because we had worked through significant self-esteem issues she had struggled with for years. Megan was the type of person who appeared strong and confident, but inside she was fragile and always questioned her self-worth.

In the privacy of my office, Megan asked me one question, a question that arises in every grief and loss crisis I deal with: "Why did this have to happen? It isn't fair!" This is a difficult question that is impossible to answer. Teenagers like answers. They like things to make sense. We all do. A teenager dying doesn't make sense. You end up talking about the fact that he was so young and he had his entire life ahead of him. We talked about memories she had and how she would live her life going forward.

As a school counselor, I can play a significant role in helping students like Megan move through the stages of grief and loss, especially when family and friends can't or are unable to provide the necessary support. This is not because they don't care; they may be grieving, too. There seems to be a certain expectation for things to return to normal as quickly as possible. The pain of grief and loss, however, is not a quick process. Grieving has a different timetable for each person and is often slow and complicated. This means that teens like Megan may take three steps forward followed by two steps back.

> The pain of grief and loss is not a quick process. Grieving has a different timetable for each person and is often slow and complicated.

It took Megan several months before she was able to move through the grief process. She has long since graduated, but we still speak of the days when she struggled over the loss of her close friend.

LAUREN

I Don't Know What to Say

One day I was suddenly called into a meeting with my fellow counselors, school administrators, and a police officer. We were informed that a student had taken his own life. He was from a different school, but his sister attended our high school, along with many of his friends.

Later that day Lauren asked to see me. I did not know her. She came to see me because her friend had suggested that she come and talk to me. I felt honored. In many respects, nothing is more important to a high school counselor than his reputation. Lauren closed the door and sat down. She showed no emotion.

Behind closed doors, Lauren was doing well with the loss of the student who took his own life. Although it shook her up, as it did all the students, she was able to cope emotionally with it. Lauren was friends with his sister and was unsure how to talk with her when she came back to school the following week. She asked, "What do I say to someone whose brother just killed himself?" Nothing is easy when working through the grief and loss process. For everyone, continuing on and resuming a normal life after a significant loss is a big challenge.

First, Lauren and I talked about the student's suicide. I told her what happened in a simple, quiet, and direct manner. It's imperative to share the truth in such situations. This is also an opportunity to dispel rumors and replace them with truth.

Lauren and I role-played some circumstances as to how she could respond. After spending some time processing this, she decided to stay true to herself by being loyal to the friendship she and the boy's sister had established. A couple of days later Lauren began by kindly asking her friend how she was doing. Lauren knew that this was necessary because everyone was already talking about the recent loss. While uncomfortable, the situation certainly could not be avoided. The brother's absence in this family's life was going to become the "new normal," and in their own way everyone would need to accept that in order to heal.

Lauren worked through her struggles related to the loss as well, and they remain friends to this day. Lauren learned that a big piece of life is learning how to deal with things that happen—especially those things that are out of her control.

TAYLOR

No One Died, but It Sure Felt Like It!

Grief and loss aren't always associated with death. There are many kinds of loss, and the emotional effect can be just as devastating, as was the case with Taylor.

Taylor was an extremely shy student, to the point that people wondered if she was afraid of interacting with people. This shyness hindered her ability to make friends because she seldom spoke with her peers, even when they tried to talk with her. This lack of friends led other students to label her as strange, and made her an easy, and therefore frequent, target for bullying.

A student named MacKenzie brought to my attention that Taylor was being bullied. I thanked her for letting me know and immediately addressed the issue with Taylor, and later with the other students involved. I continued to see Taylor regularly to make sure she was doing okay, and to help her deal with her shyness. MacKenzie also often kept me informed of any issues Taylor had with other students.

Because of this, Taylor and MacKenzie formed a special friendship that spanned almost all of high school. At first glance, you would never pick out these two as friends because they had very opposite personalities. Taylor was shy, quiet, insecure, and seen as fragile to some. MacKenzie was cold, blunt, and even harsh at times. Despite their stark differences they formed a strong bond that was strengthened by helping one another through personal hardships. For years Taylor had dealt with being victimized by bullies, leading to ongoing personal struggles and even suicidal thoughts. MacKenzie had lost her mother because of a drug overdose.

The girls became inseparable and helped each other. Taylor was a listening ear for MacKenzie, the quiet source of support as she worked through the sudden loss of her own mother. She was the shoulder that McKenzie could cry on, as she knew that all of her secrets beyond her loss, like struggling in school, were safe with Taylor.

Likewise, MacKenzie was the big sister that Taylor never had. She was always the one who would defend her and be there for her anytime anyone ever tried to bully her. MacKenzie was Taylor's voice, speaking up for her when she couldn't. She advocated for Taylor to get counseling and work through her issues.

Their friendship was perfect, or so they thought. Then one Tuesday morning things changed. MacKenzie told Taylor in an uncharacteristically quiet, nervous voice that she would be moving to Tennessee. It would happen over Christmas break, just a few weeks away. In addition to the big emotional loss they had to deal with after her mom passed away, the family experienced financial problems. MacKenzie's dad felt he needed to seek better employment. The move gave him a better chance for a promotion, which would lead to better pay, and ease their financial burden.

I spoke with them behind the closed doors of my office, together and individually. Each of them worked through anger, tears, and frustration associated with this change and how it would impact their friendship. Their plans to graduate high school together that June would not take place.

MacKenzie decided to end the relationship abruptly because she didn't want to invest in it any longer. She believed ending it this way would make it easier for both of them. She moved on, though not easily. A friendship built over years ended in virtually an instant. The decision to end the friendship, after much discussion and emotional conversation, was not mutual.

Taylor, given her quiet personality, was devastated. She was especially hurt when MacKenzie was not even willing to try to see if they could make a long-distance friendship work. She was in tears and had many issues to work through, which led her to move to outside counseling. In the end, Taylor was left to pick up the pieces of a lost friendship . . . alone.

Grief and loss looks different to different people. No one passed away, yet Taylor was still grieving. A life was not lost, yet an important relationship was. Grief and loss are not always about death and dying, but may be due to a void of some kind in one's life. It is a wound that is often difficult to mend or heal.

As teenagers, your lives are mostly ahead of you. A friend dying does not make sense, but it is a part of the life process. Losing a friend forces us to deal with the sudden and unexpected changes that we all have to face at some point. Grieving is an inevitable, unavoidable, part of the life process. It's a reminder to make us appreciate life while we have it. Take hold of the life you have.

Take hold of the life you have. Don't waste it.

> The impact you have on people can extend for generations to come.

Don't waste it. Don't act as if you don't care. Don't be apathetic. Get the most out of it. Use it. Invest it. When your life is over, people will not remember you for the things you have accumulated, they will remember you for the relationships you have with people. Material things do not last, but the impact you have on people can extend for generations to come.

Megan moved forward with her life and over time developed a true sense of self. Her loss will always be a part of her, but the loss will not define who she is because she realized that her role in this world is to make a difference. Taylor struggled to find her place right through graduation as a result of her loss. Grief and loss is a process. Overcoming the loss of a loved one (someone you care about) takes time. How you heal and the length of time it takes varies from person to person. You can't rush it, but with the support of friends, family, and others, you begin to move forward—even if only one step at a time.

POINTS TO PONDER . . .

✔ Working through the pain of grief and loss is not a quick process. Grieving has a different timetable for each person and it is often slow and complicated.

✔ Grief and loss can cause you to appreciate the life you do have, no matter how imperfect. Don't waste your life.

✔ A person does not have to die for you to feel the pain of grief and loss. Any kind of void in your life can do this. Any open wound can be difficult to mend or heal.

✔ Losing a loved one may not be fair, but it is part of the life process. It forces us to step up and deal with the sudden and unexpected changes that come with living. Has this happened to you or someone you know?

✔ There is never a wrong way to grieve through the loss of a loved one, as long as it can be done safely.

✔ At some point after a loss, you must pick yourself up and move forward. The person you lost would want you to keep living, to be a success.

Chapter 10

DRUGS AND ALCOHOL

D rug and alcohol use and abuse has risen to epidemic levels
in our country. People justify using drugs for all kinds of
reasons, from a way to relax, to a way to heal medically,
for a means to fit in socially, and even as a method to focus so one
can concentrate better to study and take high-stakes standardized
tests. Some teenagers use drugs and erroneously see them as safe
because they have parents or relatives who use them. Even if this is
not the case in a teenager's house, this perspective might also hold
true because society presents the use of many drugs and alcohol as
having benefits, and being fun, while downplaying the negative
consequences and impact.

Drug and alcohol use impacts many of the students I see. The
stories that I could share are endless because students have been

hit so hard and in such different ways. I have told my students over the years that nothing good comes from using alcohol and other drugs. I have never seen drugs and alcohol bring a mar-

I have never seen drugs and alcohol bring a marriage together and I have never seen it create unity in a family.

riage together and I have never seen it create unity in a family. Drug and alcohol use has never enhanced a relationship between a father and son, and it has never mended the bond between a

mother and daughter. With this in mind the stories that follow show that drugs and alcohol play no favorites when it comes to addiction, destruction, and despair. Victims of drug and alcohol abuse are those who use, as well as the loved ones who experience hurt because a family member uses. Numerous students of mine have come to terms with their addictions, but there are also those who are still in denial that they have a dependency even years after they have graduated, and there are also students of mine who have sadly passed away as a result. If you think you can beat the negative effects of drugs and alcohol, think again—you can't. Don't even try, you will lose.

In my office students have shed tears, vented in anger, and expressed how their hopes have been dashed—all because drugs and alcohol have impacted their lives or the lives of their family and friends. I have had to call in parents to tell them that their child shared in an English class assignment that he didn't want to live anymore because of his addiction. One student couldn't handle seeing her friend use heroin. She tried to talk her into going to rehab, yet her friend was in denial that she even had a drug problem. I also have had students make commemorative shirts, numerous times, sadly, to remember a friend and classmate who died of a drug overdose.

KELLI

Rising Above My Family's Alcohol Abuse

Despite the grip that drugs have on some students, others can and do overcome the grip that it has on an individual or family. Kelli was one of the strong and fortunate ones. She was a fighter. She wanted more out of life. She didn't want to be a statistic. She wanted better. She wanted to succeed and she did just that.

You can overcome and succeed as well. You just have to want better for your life. You can't make excuses for your addictions. You must be willing to work hard to overcome them.

Kelli was a senior. She had a 2.8 grade point average. She was friendly and worked hard in her classes, but she could have achieved so much more.

I try to meet with every student a couple of times throughout the year, but some students seek out my support more than others. Kelli would come into my office on a regular basis, really just to talk about life. I often tell my students over the course of the time that I will work with them and help prepare them for life. I am honored that they would confide in me to help shape their future. Kelli was one of those students with whom I still keep in contact today.

Kelli had a bubbly personality. She was happy and everything was always even-keeled in her world. I never saw her too high or too low. She seldom was upset, distraught, angry, or sad. But she always struck me as someone who had a back story; everything just seemed too perfect, as if she was trying to hide something. There just seemed something more to her and I was curious to find out what that was. One day I called Kelli out of her psychology class to see how she was doing. I could assess her credits toward graduation as well as discuss college and her plans moving forward. Kelli arrived and I closed the door. I almost always close the door. I figure no one else needs to know what is going on with my students, even if we are not in a discussion about something troubling. I reviewed her credits, college plans, and so much more. Everything she shared gave me more respect for her than almost any student I have had over the years.

> I asked Kelli in a casual manner, "Every time I see you, you are so positive and upbeat. Would you agree with that?"
>
> Kelli responded: "Yeah, I am."
>
> "Did you get that skill from your parents? You live with just your dad, right?"
>
> "Yes, I live with just my dad now, but I don't get it from him."
>
> I inquired: "Where does it come from?"
>
> "Me," Kelli responded in such a matter-of-fact way.
>
> "You live with your dad, but you didn't get your positive outlook from him. . . . What's your dad like?"
>
> "You really want to know?"
>
> "If you're willing to share, I'm more than willing to listen."

That was the start of a journey with Kelli that would last from the end of her junior year right through graduation. Kelli reminded me that even when you think you know a student, you may not. She had such a skill to allow circumstances to just deflect off, seldom if ever having an impact on her. She is simply a tremendous person. She is a model of resiliency and she also exhibits the power of perseverance that exists within all of us. It exists within all of us only if we are willing to understand that we have it and want to learn how to use it. This is how we can unleash ourselves to reach our ultimate potential.

Kelli lived with both of her parents when she was born, but as she approached her preschool years her parents often argued, which would escalate into yelling and often door-slamming. Much of their conflict was built on a foundation of drug use for her mom and alcohol for her dad. Kelli told me that she couldn't remember a time when they *weren't* drinking or using; it had always been an issue that impacted their home. The constant arguing ultimately led to a separation. Kelli grew up living between her mom's and dad's houses where drugs and alcohol continued to consume their lives. As the divorce became final, she chose to live with her dad. Kelli's mom was too far gone on drugs and was unable to appropriately care for herself, let alone care for Kelli. The judge's decision was that she could live with her dad, but that he had to cease drinking in order to provide a healthy environment for Kelli. Her dad agreed to these terms and so she lived with him full time.

I asked Kelli how her dad had done over the years with these restrictions placed on him by the court. Kelli said that he did terribly. She told me that he drank the same day that he was given custody of her after they left the courthouse. Kelli can remember days where her dad would be passed out on the couch from drinking excessive amounts of alcohol. I was so amazed at how she was able to handle seeing this, day in and day out. Kelli can remember her dad drinking a twelve-pack in an afternoon. She has even seen him on multiple occasions drink eighteen or twenty-four beers in one evening while watching football games on television.

"Kelli, why didn't you report it? You could have received some help," I asked.

She told me that she knew she could never report it or say anything to anyone because she always remembered what the judge said.

"What did the judge say?" I inquired.

Kelli answered, "The judge said that if my dad failed I would wind up in foster care. That was the last thing I wanted to have happen." Kelli knew that foster care could not guarantee her the outcome that she wanted. She felt that it was too risky because she believed that all foster care homes are not great places and she would lose all control of her circumstances. Her goal was to graduate from high school and make a life of her own. She was not going to let her family dysfunction hinder her personal ambitions.

Over several weeks, Kelli would come to my office. She was so willing to open her world to me. I truly felt so honored to get a glimpse of what she dealt with every day. I wondered how she did it. I recall our conversation as to how she managed to deal with how drugs and alcohol impacted her family. She said this and I found it so profound: "I can't make my parents stop using, but I can choose how I respond to it." What a mature reply! What a testimony of personal effort to overcome adversity.

> She could have made excuses for her parents, but she recognized that she could not change their behavior. She focused on what she could control, which was her school work and her plans for a life all her own.

She could have let her circumstances get the best of her. She probably could have become an alcohol or drug addict herself, but if you talked to her she always wanted better for herself. College was always Kelli's goal; graduation was her ticket to get there. Nothing was going to stop her from making that happen. She could have made excuses for her parents, but she recognized that she could not change their behavior. She focused on what she could control, which was her school work and her plans for a life all her own.

Today, while her parents continue to struggle with addictions and the resentment over their marriage, Kelli gets ready to graduate from college, ready to create for herself—one day at a time—the life she always wanted. She wanted a stable and safe home filled with love and security instead of anger, alcohol, and drugs.

ASHLEY

Because It's Fun!

Teenagers, unfortunately, more often times than not, make the same bad choices their parents do when it comes to drugs and alcohol. Unlike Kelli, Ashley was one who always made the wrong choice for herself. Drugs, alcohol, sex and any combination of the three was what Ashley was all about. She loved to drink, especially on the weekends. She always seemed to want to live on the edge.

Ashley's parents were divorced. Both struggled financially. Her dad always seemed to move from one apartment to the next, floundering in life socially even though he had a good-paying job.

Ashley followed the example that was modeled to her. She drank on the weekend at parties and mixed in some marijuana for some added "fun," as she called it. She had average grades when she was in high school, but was capable of much more. Her parents were divorced most of her life. She used drugs, alcohol, and sex to fill the voids of love and security that her parents never gave her. She got along with both her parents well, but she never felt like she could be honest with them about life and the challenges of growing up because she wanted to protect the image that they had of her.

I had worked with Ashley for years. We would chat about her life, her fears, and her expectations for her future—you name it, we talked about it. Behind closed doors during one of our conversations, I asked her the following:

"Ashley, you use drugs without thinking of the consequences, have sex without considering the ramifications, and drink away your worries. You are smart enough to know better before you do it [she agreed], so why do you live as you do and make the choices you do?"

Ashley responded: "Because the fun is too fun to walk away from . . . the high covers up all of the pain."

"Would you want to be happy without needing the high and promiscuous lifestyle?" I asked.

"It's no big deal. I guess I would just rather live for the moment, be carefree . . . Mr. K, really . . . I'm good."

She was really never willing to work on the quality of her life. I have learned over the years that you cannot help someone work through their personal struggles and problems unless they take the first step and admit that they actually have problems. The road leading you to temptation always has a path leading *away* from it. Yes, it takes courage and bravery to make the tough choice, but in the end it's the path with the fewest damaging consequences—if any.

> The road leading you to temptation always has a path leading *away* from it.

AARON

A Bad Decision Was His Final Decision

While I was on a family Christmas vacation in Miami, I got a phone call that a student of mine named Aaron had died of a drug overdose. I stood on our balcony looking at the vast Atlantic Ocean. It was peaceful, beautiful, but I felt anything but calm. A whirlwind of emotions came over me, thinking of Aaron, a senior who had his whole life ahead of him—all wasted because of a bad decision to drink excessively at a late-night party. Aaron was a sharp student who was all set to attend a university in the fall. He planned to study accounting and finance. He had no known substance-abuse problems. This was not typical behavior for him and he seldom went to parties let alone drank at them.

I tell my students that nothing good happens between 11 PM and 6 AM. Teenagers should go home and stay home. When you hang out with the wrong crowd, bad things are more likely to happen even if you don't want them to. If this advice had been followed, Aaron might still be with us today.

> Nothing good happens between 11 PM and 6 AM

Tragically, his family ended up planning his funeral instead of his graduation party. Their lives would never be the same again. Sadly, Aaron was not the first student of mine who passed away because of drugs; unfortunately he likely won't be the last one. The number of teens dying from drug overdoses and abuse now exceeds the number of deaths from motor vehicle accidents in the U.S.[4]

4 http://kfor.com/2013/08/30/teen-drug-overdose-deaths-surpass-car-accident.deaths-in-u-s/

Kelli, Ashley, and Aaron: three students with issues of drugs and alcohol, but with very different responses and outcomes. Drugs and alcohol are only a means to avoid greater issues in a person's life. Ironically, people often use them to cope, to feel better, but in the end, their use only complicates things. Under the influence, people lose their inhibitions, and do and say things they might never consider with a clear head. One night of abuse can lead to a lifetime of addiction, or, in some cases, death.

Drug and alcohol abuse are merciless; they cause teenagers to lose their sense of reality. All teens make mistakes—this is normal, a part of growing up. Unfortunately, mistakes brought on by drugs and alcohol may not be easily fixed. Whether you are an upper-classman, a 4.0 student, from the inner city, from a wealthy family in the affluent suburbs, struggling with finding enough food to eat, or one of the star athletes in your high school, drugs and alcohol do not discriminate. They impact all demographics, cities, and communities. No one is immune from the effects and nothing good comes from active drug use and abuse.

> No one is immune from the effects and nothing good comes from active drug use and abuse.

Life is all about the choices we make each day and the ramifications of those choices. Making responsible choices despite temptations ultimately makes the challenges of growing up much easier to manage. Popular media, such as movies, music, and advertisements, portray drug and alcohol use as fun. Don't believe it. It's not fun and it's filled with consequences that lead down a road filled with setbacks and negativity. No advertisement or movie

> Life is all about the choices we make each day and the ramifications of those choices.

shows us the teenager passed out, throwing up in the bushes at a party, or dead from an overdose. Behind closed doors I have seen this reality. I've spoken with parents who called the police on their own children because they kept stealing from them to support their addiction.

> No advertisement or movie shows us the teenager passed out, throwing up in the bushes at a party, or dead from an overdose.

I've listened to the sister who strives every day to do her best, but gets no attention from her parents because they are so focused on dealing with their son's alcohol addiction. I've seen the destruction of lives because of drugs and alcohol, as well as those teenagers who have worked hard to recover—but who are still dealing with the scars of substance abuse.

I've had students willingly go to rehab to try and deal with their issues and move forward in a positive manner, but I've also attended the funerals of parents and students because of substance abuse. Some were because of addictions over years, others because everything went wrong just one time.

Teenagers who use illegal substances almost always use with other teenagers. Choose your friends wisely. Your so-called "friends" may appear to have good intentions, but their influence could lead you down a dangerous road. Real friends

> Choose your friends wisely. Your so-called "friends" may appear to have good intentions, but their influence could lead you down a dangerous road.

are trustworthy, honest, and loyal. They have your back, protecting you and looking out for your best interests especially when you become blinded by temptation or peer pressure. They stand by you when things are going well, and when you are going through the worst of times.

Surrounding yourself with positive people is one of the best ways to ensure that you will make responsible choices. So if you are at a party and someone asks you to try alcohol or drugs, you need to know how you will respond. What would you do? What would you say? Would you flee? Would you panic and try it to fit in? Would you laugh it off to avoid the situation? My suggestion: say nothing and walk away. No explanation is needed. You don't have to justify your actions, just stay true to your morals and convictions. It may not be an easy choice to make in the midst of peers, but it is the safest one. Making wise decisions is not always simple, but thinking about your friends, family, and the future that lies ahead of you can help make the decisions you face (including issues of drugs and alcohol) a little easier to manage.

POINTS TO PONDER...

✔ Nothing good comes from drug and alcohol use. It will not bring a marriage together, re-create unity in a family, or enhance a bond between parent and child.

✔ There are no winners in the dangerous game of drugs and alcohol. Play this game once and it could ruin your life, if not kill you.

✔ You can't force someone to stop using drugs and alcohol, but you can control how you choose to respond to it.

✔ Every road to temptation has a path leading away from it. How do you avoid the world of teenage drug and alcohol abuse when temptations to experiment with illicit substances are everywhere?

✔ Nothing good happens between 11 PM and 6 AM.

✔ Drugs and alcohol are used by people to escape personal struggles within their lives. In reality, they never remedy a struggle and ultimately only further complicate things.

✔ Life is all about the choices we make each day and the ramifications of those choices. The choices you make about drugs and alcohol are no exception.

Chapter 11

DATING AND SEX

Magazines, movies, music—they all in one way or another promote sex as fun with no consequences. Almost every day, kids come in to see me and behind closed doors talk about their sexual activity. Teenagers seek guidance regarding sex because, as they come to realize, there are indeed consequences and there is no such thing as a casual hook-up or a simple friend with benefits.

I'm amazed over the years at the promiscuous lifestyles of teenagers and how they get themselves into such complicated situations, including dating relationships that resulted in a pregnancy or sexually transmitted disease (STD). More often than not I have seen how self-esteem is often tied to one's sexual activity, especially for girls.

KARI

Feeling Used!

Kari, a junior, is a student whom I have seen probably dozens of times over her high school years. Usually, she would just show up at my office door during her lunch hour to talk about relationship struggles. Today was no exception. She is a poster child for both the devaluing of women in relationships and the ease with which men have access to sex.

I believe that the attitude toward having sex has been evolving over the past several years. Our attitudes have shifted from one of waiting for sex until one is older or married to an attitude of curious early experimentation. A perspective as to why this occurred is important because history often repeats itself, and the views toward sex today must be understood and looked at more honestly so you can learn and not repeat the same mistakes. The result is a revolution of sorts in how men and women date and how sex takes its place in the relationship. I believe that for men, the availability of sex in noncommitted relationships has taken away one key reason why men used to marry. Women now engage in sexual relationships while still in the dating stage, in an effort to increase the commitment level of the guy. The reality is that the guy is getting what he wanted without any need for him to invest or commit to the relationship. Not that men could not get sex in decades past; I just think that people had to date longer prior to it. Today, in a sexually charged society, high school girls have sex hoping to secure a boy's commitment when at one time that security was found mostly through getting married. Kari dealt with something similar to this.

Spending much time behind closed doors with students like Kari has allowed me to notice trends: issues that occur more often than others. One of the trends is a warped sense of self-worth in a dating relationship. This is experienced when a student (like Kari) seldom expresses her opinions in the relationship. Instead she always follows the wishes of her date. She never stands up for what she believes in or feels, and uses having sex as a way to feel valued. If you struggle with issues related to self-worth or self-esteem, I encourage you to talk with your parents, school counselor, or social worker, or find a licensed therapist in your area who can help you work through this.

I was told by another student that Kari had recently been dumped by her boyfriend. I called her down right after school started, at 7:30 in the morning. Sitting in my office, she seemed numb, still, and emotionless, staring at the floor. Although it was early, this had nothing to do with trying to wake up.

> Closing the door, I attempted to break through. "Kari, how are you?" I said.
>
> "Okay," she responded.
>
> "Kari, I heard that you and Greg broke up. What happened?"
>
> With a puzzled look Kari said, "He likes someone else, but he said that it's not that he doesn't like me."
>
> "What did he like about someone else?" I inquired.
>
> "Do you really want to know why?" Kari asked.
>
> "I only want to know if you want to tell me," I said.
>
> Kari stated in a quiet tone, "He wanted to know if the sex in a new relationship is better than what he has with me."
>
> "How does it make you feel to hear that from Greg?"
>
> "Used!"

Kari was one of those high school girls that any guy would consider himself lucky to be dating. She was kind, sweet, loyal as can be, and to top it off she was a bright student. She was one of those people who seemed to have everything going for her both in school and socially. Missing from her life, however, was a sense of self-worth. While she should have been proud about her accomplishments and who she was becoming as a person, she was constantly trying to please others, at her own expense, to gain self-acceptance.

Kari was faithful and loyal, which are admirable character traits, but not when you sacrifice yourself in the process. In many ways, Kari's "nice" personality was something that people took advantage of. She seemed to have low expectations of other people, and her boyfriend was no exception. Kari was only about a month into her relationship with Greg when she decided to have sex with him. She rationalized this by saying that she wanted to show him that she was committed to their relationship, and the two of them sleeping together showed Greg that Kari really cared.

As time passed I got to spend time with Greg as well. He was an average student at best who shared with me that sex was an issue in their relationship. Not that it was bad, but he wanted to see what it was like to have sex with someone else. Greg wanted to know if the grass was greener on the other side, as they say. While Kari was focused on the emotional side of the relationship, Greg's focus was solely on the physical aspects. He cared about Kari and wanted to see her do well in life, but his selfish desires were more important than having a relationship with her.

In my countless hours spent with teenagers over the years, I've seen a lot of unhealthy dating relationships and a lack of appropriate values regarding sex. Sex among teenagers has become almost a requirement in dating. This sexual revolution along with the use of technology and social media has sabotaged the fun and fascinating aspects of getting to know someone through face to face, nonsexual interaction. So many teenage relationships are based on the physical aspects with minimal investment being made on the relational and emotional components. Plus, the ease of access to and prevalence of pornography and sexualized images have caused teenage girls to feel as if they have to act in a sexual manner in order to be noticed. Kari fell into this trap. This all but eliminates the likelihood of the relationship being authentic, and ultimately traps girls rather than empowering them.

> The ease of access to and prevalence of pornography and sexualized images have caused teenage girls to feel as if they have to act in a sexual manner in order to be noticed.

Many adults and teenagers believe that high school is a time for self-exploration through dating. Going out with someone, to the movies, to dinner, to football games, etc., provides opportunities for growth in learning about yourself as well as the person you are dating. You can find out who you are as a person and also what you want and don't want in a spouse later on in life. It seems that for Kari and many other girls, dating is not an activity undertaken to explore oneself; instead, it is for seeking validation and the need to be liked, they have sex and give up their self-worth in return. To stop this mindset, teenagers must be honest with themselves and determine the level of character and integrity that they want for their lives. Some teenagers may want to seek out an adult they trust or a mentor in an effort to help them work through this.

Many students develop a curiosity toward sex, in part due to puberty, but primarily due to media saturation that encourages students to engage in sex. Additionally, some teenagers have sex to satisfy their own needs. Some do this by choice while others do this as a means to gain the love and attention that they are not receiving from family and loved ones at home.

Kari found that there is no substitute for time when investing in a relationship. Sex often becomes a tool that is used to speed up or try to strengthen the relationship. This is hardly the result. In actuality, sex only complicates dating and cannot strengthen a relationship because real relationships are built in time on trust, respect, integrity, and character. Sex at a young age, in the absence of a mature foundation and marital commitment, can create the baggage of anger, resentment, and insecurity. This leads to additional physical and emotional issues that are seldom, if ever, dealt with, and thus the same mistakes are made again and again. Sex makes you vulnerable. If you don't have a strong sense of self-worth and some standards to support it, in the end sex will leave you feeling used and empty. Remember if you do what the world does, you'll get what the world gets. Engaging in sex while dating brings about long-term consequences. Most people would do almost anything to be able to go back and undo sexual relationships that have caused them so much pain.

> Engaging in sex while dating brings about long-term consequences. Most people would do almost anything to be able to go back and undo sexual relationships that have caused them so much pain.

CAMDEN

No Means No!

Over the years, I have dealt far more frequently with girls than boys on issues related to sex and dating. I think this is because girls are more in touch with their emotions and often have a need to talk through and process things in the hope of gaining clarity about their the situation, whereas guys typically hold things in and try to manage things themselves. This could be because of pride and not wanting to bother someone else with their issues, or because they believe that they can best handle their problems unassisted.

Camden was a tenth-grade student to see me because his girl-friend was a student of mine. Camden, unfortunately, was a strug-gling student academically. He was one who most people would classify as below average since he typically earned grades of C− or lower. He had the ability to do better, but struggled to put forth consistent effort in the classroom each day or turn in his home-work on time.

Camden showed up to my office on a dreary October morning. Standing in the doorway to my office he looked dejected, almost numb. He looked like he was hurting, yet he also seemed confused and lost—as though he were in a daze. I told him to come in, close the door, and sit down so we could talk about what was going on.

"Hi, Camden. It's good to see you. Is there something I can help you with?"

Camden replied in a curious manner: "You know Annie [his girl-friend], don't you?"

I replied: "I can't tell you anything about Annie. Why do you ask?"

"Well, she told me that she talked to you and I wanted you to know that she broke up with me yesterday."

Empathetically I responded: "I'm sorry to hear that, what happened?"

"Well . . . we have been dating for a couple of weeks and I wanted to sleep with her, you know, have sex with her, but she didn't want to. I continued to ask but she kept saying no. This time when I asked she dumped me!" Camden said.

"Okay, Camden, thanks for sharing and being so honest. Why do you think she broke up with you?" I wanted to hear what his take on it was.

Looking confused and bewildered, Camden replied: "I don't know."

"Camden, you wanted to sleep with her and the answers you got were no, no, and no! She never said maybe, or, let me think about it. She was very clear with her response to your advances, would you agree?"

Embarrassed, Camden replied: "Yeah."

"So, considering this, why did you guys break up?" I asked.

Camden, with tears welling up in his eyes, replied just as they began to stream down his face: "Because I didn't listen to what she said."

I responded: "You're right. You didn't listen to her . . . you didn't respect her wishes and what she wanted. She wanted to be respected and you were unable to do that, so she ended it."

"Mr. K," Camden said.

"Yeah, Camden."

"Can I tell you something?"

"You can tell me anything. If you're willing to tell me . . . I'm willing to listen. What's on your mind?"

Camden replied: "My last three relationships have ended like this. I really liked Annie. She was cute, fun, and made me laugh. I have never had someone teach me how to treat a girl, what I should do or say."

"What about your dad?" I asked.

"My dad only sees me a couple of times a year at the most. He barely knows who I am. I'm not talking to my mom about this; that would be embarrassing."

The pressure to have sex in high school is there and that pressure varies depending on the social group one is a part of. Staying true to who you are is critical to your ability to manage these pressures.

Over the years I can't tell you how often I talk to teenage boys and deal with issues similar to Camden's. Camden was trying to do the best he could. He saw a girl whom he liked, who he thought was cute. What did he do? He pursued her. He just went about it the wrong way.

I find more and more teenage boys like Camden who have no one to mentor them through the process of how to treat a girl. More often than not they pursue a girl in a manner consistent with what they hear from their friends. In talking with Camden, I found that he learned about how to date a girl from his friends and really no one else. His experiences with friends about dating had nothing to do with how a guy should *treat* a girl; it had everything to do with what he should *get* from a girl. His experiences (with his friends) as well as with media influences told him that his interactions with a girl should be focused on the physical so that is what he pursued with Annie—and ultimately what led to disappointment.

More and more frequently I deal with students who don't live with their father or don't have a dad who is a vital part of their life. I have had some students who have a father at home, but that person struggles to invest in them. There are numerous amazing fathers who do everything needed to raise strong, mature, respectful young men. For those who don't have a father in their life to fulfill that role, I encourage you to seek out a mentor to help you with the issue of dating and treating a girl well (and topics beyond that). A mentor might be an uncle, grandpa, teacher, or other trusted adult, but it ought to be someone you look up to as a role model.

Guys—treat girls with respect and value them as people. Girls—demand to be treated well because you deserve it. Expectations drive every dating relationship. These expectations are established because of values and standards that you have as to what you deserve or how you should be treated. Respecting each other is nonnegotiable. You must both give respect to your date and expect it back in return. Respect provides a foundation in your dating experiences that allows you to learn what you want now in a date and eventually in a future mate.

> Guys—treat girls with respect and value them as people. Girls—demand to be treated well because you deserve it.

BRANDI

Dating with the Future in Mind

A senior named Brandi shared a conversation with me that I have had with many other students. She had sex with her boyfriend after they had been dating for several months and later that *same day* he dumped her because he decided he just "wasn't into" the relationship.

> "What did you learn from this experience, Brandi?" I asked.
>
> "Aside from feeling used and confused?" Brandi responded, adding, "I learned that I have a lot of growing up to do."
>
> "What do you mean by that?" I continued.
>
> Brandi responded, "I learned that I can't date like I am in high school. I am off to college in a few months. I need to date with my future in mind because I am more likely to find a quality guy when he is focused on his future too."

Dating is a learning experience, and calls for maturity and self-awareness. Getting to know someone in this way allows you to understand what you want—and don't want—in a relationship. I have *never* seen a healthy dating relationship for teenagers that focuses on sex as a vital component. Sex among teenagers is an epidemic, and we must look at it as a problem and not simply a generational change in values. Teenagers who are serious about dating should be respectful of each other. Despite all of the emotions you feel, work slowly into the relationship because there is no substitute for time. Maturity is knowing who you are and who you are not. Maturity is the willingness to pass up immediate pleasure for long-term gain. You have to know who you are as a person before you can ever know what you want in a girlfriend or boyfriend. Having sex while dating in high school only minimizes self-worth, and creates a false sense of security that the relationship will last forever. Don't allow temporary physical

> Maturity is the willingness to pass up immediate pleasure for long-term gain.

gratification to cloud your judgment from what you really value. Sex within the confines of marriage is safe and secure because two adults are committed to one another to live life together "till death do us part."

When it comes to sex, I believe that parents, communities, and society as a whole have done a poor job of educating teens about the consequences of engaging in intimate relationships. Parents, it seems, at best had a one-time conversation with you about sex, which most commonly was done (if at all) because of body changes one goes through during puberty and early teenage years. Many parents are then relieved that this conversation is over with and is never relived again.

Teenagers grow up confused about their hormones while being curious about sex at the same time. Your brains are still developing and unable to process these feelings, which results in unanswered questions about sex. Many times, no regular dialogue takes place at home to process these feelings. Many parents and societal expectations only want to ensure their child doesn't become pregnant or get someone pregnant. I once had someone tell me that being pregnant in high school is like your parents grounding you for eighteen years! Teenagers, for the most part understand this consequence of sex, but communication through conversation is the key. Teenagers want to know what their parents think about sex even though it is embarrassing to discuss. Although teenagers learn more from their peers about sex than from adults, the information is often inaccurate. Parents and teenagers must get past

> Teenagers want to know what parents think about sex even though it is embarrassing to discuss.

the fear and awkwardness and have healthy meaningful conversations about sex and life in general.

Some teenagers grow up with parents saying nothing about sex, while their peers and the media—primarily music, movies, and television—speak constantly of how great sex is, while never once considering the emotional impact that having sex can have on the life of a teen. Being curious about sex is normal and it doesn't make you a "dirty" person, but when those feelings are acted upon it complicates life and creates major distractions that often sidetrack you from your goals. My experience has shown me that teenagers primarily learn about sex through their peers, experimentation, and pornography. These influences lead to false information and inaccurate expectations.

Even in a world where society promotes sex as gratification with no strings attached, even if it *seems* like everyone else is having sex and you don't want to feel like the odd person out, stop and think before you act. Momentary pleasure has consequences—and they can last a lifetime.

The foundation of a healthy dating relationship is established through getting to know another person, not for the physical interactions you can have with the person you are dating. The reason this is important is because when teenagers experiment with sex while dating and the relationship ends, sexual baggage is carried to the next dating relationship. This means that if a teenager's past sexual experiences were embarrassing, painful, unfulfilling, or humiliating—to name a few—it heightens the anxiety and trust issues leading into the next relationship. These issues make having a future successful relationship much more complicated because of the baggage that is brought to it. This leads most commonly to unresolved struggles of self-worth, and not feeling able to measure up.

Behind closed doors, teenagers ask me all the time how to keep a relationship flourishing in the midst of the hectic pace of high school. I find myself telling teenagers that they need to focus on the strong points of the relationship, and if the conflict is great then it may be time to end the relationship. Too many times, I've seen teenage girls stay with a guy for the wrong reasons. They may feel an obligation to be with him because of their reputation, so their peers won't think less of them because they can't keep a relationship, or because of the sexual decisions they have made. It may also be for the sake of security in that they don't want to be alone or they want to "change" their boyfriend because they see potential in him.

> If you have made poor choices in relationships, making more bad choices will only compound your problems.

If you have made poor choices in relationships, making more bad choices will only compound your problems. There's a line from the movie *Jerry Maguire*, where Jerry (Tom Cruise) tells Dorothy (Renée Zellweger) "... you complete me." Nothing could be further from the truth. Successful relationships ought to *improve* who you are as a person, *not complete* or define you. People come and go in our lives. We need to be complete and *then* enter into a relationship.

> Successful relationships ought to *improve* who you are as a person, *not complete* or define you.

Sex simply complicates dating relationships; it does not make them successful. Too many times I have seen girls in my office who believe that sex within a relationship shows your commitment to the relationship, when it typically only reflects the poor quality of the guy you date. Do you really want to settle for less than you deserve?

My advice to teenage girls is the same today as it was when I first started counseling: Find a guy who will treat you like a princess—*now!* You deserve this kind of treatment. The person you date is the person you will get if you marry. You will not change that person's personality. This is a lesson that even adults often do not learn, and why so many marriages often end in divorce. If you understand this now, however, you will be more likely to find that great guy later. This is imperative for girls to understand because it demonstrates that the guy likes and respects them for who they are as a person, and not just for the sexual favors, the immediate gratification, that they can receive from their girlfriend. Confidence will go a long way in your dating experience in high school. It allows you to stay true to who you are as a person and realize the value of being honest and authentic with someone else.

JESSICA

Desperate for Security

Everyone has struggles and internal conflicts. That is just part of life, but these things can be magnified when you are a teenager because you are at that place between childhood and full adulthood. You might look and feel like an adult, but you still don't have the life experience that an adult has, and with it the true ability to process many thoughts and feelings.

Jessica was an eleventh-grade student, like many, who was striving to grow up in a society filled with challenges and a home life that was crumbling. Her parents were on the brink of divorce. The yelling between them was almost an everyday occurrence. She had been dating her boyfriend for about six months, but she had no one whom she could talk to about life, let alone the more serious subjects of dating and sex.

In my interactions with her, I got to know a fragile girl who had a difficult time expressing her struggles verbally. She was shy and quiet and had very few friends. She often knew what she wanted to say, but didn't know how to verbalize it. This is not unusual, and oftentimes students can better express themselves at home, by themselves, where they don't feel self-conscious. In these cases, I ask them, as I did Jessica, to journal about their thoughts and feelings on paper as best as they can and bring it back to my office the next day. Jessica did just that and returned the next day with her journal entry. It paints a clear picture of the struggles that teenagers go through in dealing with dating and the temptations of sex. It allows us to see the tug-of-war that students go through in their heads, and that they lack skills to process these powerful feelings appropriately. Jessica wrote:

I'm lying in bed wishing Justin was next to me keeping me warm. I can't wait to get married to him someday. We can have our own house and kids and wake up every morning together. Tomorrow when he comes over I am going to be so hyper. I can honestly say I hope we don't just make out. This time, I hope we go all the way.

I feel like I can make my own choices when it comes to this. Do I wish I could tell my parents about this? Yeah, of course, because I could get more protection! Justin made sure I was comfortable with everything going on. He was so worried about me and my feelings that he forgot about himself. My parents wouldn't understand all of this, that is why I am writing all of my feelings in here because if I didn't express myself, I would explode. This is my only relief . . .

Jessica chose immediate gratification over long-term gain. What we should understand is not simply her choice, but the internal conflict she had about her decision, and that clearly comes through in her writing. She was obviously worried and fearful, and she proceeded to justify her decision to have sex as a component of the dating relationship. She *wanted* to tell her parents, but she felt she *couldn't* tell them. She was worried about getting pregnant, too. Consider this: if having sex is such a great thing to do, shouldn't you be able to tell everyone about it, especially your parents? If it does not feel right, it probably isn't.

Dating and opening your heart up to another is always risky, but the risk feels greater in high school. If the relationship is going well everything seems wonderful, but as soon as conflicts arise, mutual interest and happiness is replaced by turmoil and heartache. The joys of dating are minimized and the risks of dating become realized. Life is full of challenges; dating is just one of them. Putting yourself out there to trust someone with your heart is difficult, but it is the only way you truly grow in dating. Dating helps you see those character traits that you want in a potential mate. Growth occurs while dating when two people desire to get to know one another, seeking to find out those things that they have in common. Dating allows you to see who you are as a person and helps you find someone who is compatible with you.

Are you willing to make choices that resist physical advances? Our initial physical attraction to someone is almost always driven by hormones—this is a documented, scientific fact—which gives us the "butterflies," "walking on clouds" feelings, the belief that "I can't live without" the other person. While this served a biological purpose—to meet, mate, and procreate—we should be governed by more than our hormones. We have brains, we should use them. Our hormone levels naturally level out and we always come down from the clouds. True and lasting love comes from really getting to know someone. When you hear people in long-lasting relationships they talk about being married to their best friend. This is the way it should be. Your true friends never devalue you, or make you do something you don't want to do. They are with you because of the *totality* of you.

First and foremost, you must be your own best friend. If you don't love who you are and value your own body then you will pay the price for the quality of the guy or girl you date, and accept the consequences that come along with "loving" him or her.

Many parents only consider the consequences of a pregnant teenager. In truth, the emotional impact goes so much deeper than that. Remember, the sexual situations portrayed on television shows or in movies are not real; that is why they call it entertainment. Television never shows the consequences of sex because that would be a *true* reality show.

Choices have consequences and sex within the confines of dating complicates your ability to know who you really are and minimizes your ability to assess the quality of the person you are dating. Behind my office doors, way too many students have wished they had chosen to abstain from sex because the emotional impact is far greater than they ever could have imagined. Jillian and Abby are two of those students—though they represent so many—who expressed their regrets to me.

JILLIAN

I'll Never Do That Again!

Jillian was a freshman whom I saw many times over several weeks. She'd had sex with her boyfriend and was terrified because she missed her period. Looking at her calendar and when she'd had sex she calculated that it was highly possible she was pregnant. After much discussion with me, she decided to share what was going on with her parents.

They were clearly upset. "That is not how we raised you!" they said. However, they loved their daughter unconditionally and they gave her the utmost care and support. Her parents really could not have handled it any better. Jillian had a look of relief on her face as if the weight of the world had been lifted up off her shoulders. Despite multiple pregnancy tests that came back negative, with every passing day that she didn't get her period, she assumed that she was pregnant. She was getting ready to go to the doctor one morning when her period finally started—five weeks late.

Days later, Jillian and I spoke about her circumstances. She said, "At the time, having sex with my boyfriend felt like the right thing to do. It seemed natural; besides, everyone else was having sex. If I could go back and do things over again I would do them much differently. I got very lucky! Having sex was too risky. Never again will I have sex until I get married!"

Jillian's fears were eliminated, but her views on having sex had changed drastically—forever. She knew she was fortunate, and only then realized her mistake. Unfortunately, Abby did not have the same outcome.

ABBY

There Is No Such Thing as Safe Sex!

Abby was a senior who had a boyfriend for a little over a year. After they had been sexually active for a few months, one night of unprotected sex resulted in an unexpected pregnancy.

Abby was angry and upset about the pregnancy and how it would affect her future, so she considered an abortion or putting up the baby for adoption. Her boyfriend was neither helpful nor supportive. Accepting no responsibility for his part in this situation, he fumed at Abby when she told him about the pregnancy. He blamed her and told her he was sure that she wanted to get pregnant on purpose just so she could have the baby she always wanted. He used this as an excuse to end the relationship, leaving Abby to deal with this situation on her own while he went off and resumed his life as though nothing ever happened.

Reluctantly, she sat her parents down and told them about her pregnancy. They were upset, angry, and demanded that she have an abortion for fear that the pregnancy would hurt the reputation of the family. Abby did not honor the wishes of her parents because of her religious beliefs. Rather than support her and deal with the situation at hand, they forced her to move hundreds of miles away to live with a family friend who was willing to take her in for the duration of her pregnancy.

A year later, Abby was an unexpected visitor to my office. She came to give me an update about what had happened over the past year. She shared with me that, after much conflict, discussion, and tears she and her family had reconciled. They supported Abby, who was now a single mom at age eighteen. Her son's father remained absent.

While she now has her family back, it is important to realize what Abby sacrificed by acting on impulse and passion instead of with patience and maturity. She forfeited her senior year of high school—no homecoming, no prom, no graduation ceremony. While the rest of her friends will go to college, and discover what career path they want to take, she will be responsible for raising her son. If she does go to college, it will be at night and take far longer than it would have if she were able to focus on just her education.

It is one thing to sacrifice for your children when you are an adult, but quite another when you are still a teen. Abby will sacrifice *years*—time, events, and experiences that she will never be able to get back—all because of a few *minutes* of physical pleasure. Her child will sacrifice, too.

Even though Abby practiced safe sex most of the time, no birth control method is foolproof. The safest sex is *no* sex. Some people say that it is unrealistic for teenagers to abstain, but remember that sex begins with choices based on values and ends with consequences. Abby said, "I love my baby, but I wish I would have waited for sex. Sex is not for teenagers. I thought I was ready for it, but I was so mistaken. Teenagers think they are ready, when they have no idea what they are talking about."

> No birth control method is foolproof. The safest sex is *no* sex.

Jillian and Abby experienced the consequences of sex. Too many times teenagers do not think first; instead, they follow their hormones and live for the moment. Seriously consider the morals and values you have surrounding dating and premarital sex. Set standards for yourself and stay true to them. You have your whole life and a world of opportunity ahead of you; don't throw that away for someone else or for your own physical desires. The consequences of sex go far beyond getting pregnant. They are emotional, mental, physical, and even spiritual for some. These are issues that you will carry with you to your next relationship. Value yourself. Invest in your future. Save the sex for marriage when you know that you have the commitment and responsibility that comes along with it.

I've found that if you were raised with no consequences for inappropriate behavior, you believe that there are no consequences. You don't see the consequences until the poor choices have already been made. Setting boundaries for yourself allows you to date without regret. Value yourself and insist on being treated the way you deserve to be treated: with respect. These standards allow you to plan for a future, and realize your potential both in your personal relationships and in life.

> Setting boundaries for yourself allows you to date without regret. Value yourself and insist on being treated the way you deserve to be treated: with respect.

POINTS TO PONDER . . .

✔ Having sex while dating in high school minimizes self-worth and creates insecurity. Don't allow temporary physical desires to cloud your judgment.

✔ What should a healthy dating relationship look like?

✔ What are your values regarding sex? How do you stay true to those standards?

✔ Dating without sex allows you to see who you are as a person and helps you determine your level of compatability with them.

✔ Sex is often used to speed up or strengthen a relationship, when in fact it only creates baggage, anger, resentment, and insecurity.

✔ What have you learned about dating relationships from your parents? Was it good or bad? How has this influenced how you view dating?

✔ To whom do you have to keep yourself accountable in your dating relationships regarding sex? How do you set boundaries in dating and how do you stay true to them?

Chapter 12

ESTABLISHING A CAREER

While teenagers talk about how they can't wait to leave school, live on their own, and make their own money and decisions, the truth is that finding a job, one that you love, is not easy. It takes perseverance and lots of hard work—and even more hard work to stay there. Why? Because quality paying jobs can be scarce, with many others seeking the same jobs that you desire.

College graduates often believe that they deserve an excellent paying job because they have a college degree. In reality, even with a college degree, at best they only deserve the *opportunity* to apply for a job.

Some of you may be undecided about your career plans. This is fine. Let me reassure you that you are not alone in your uncertainty about the future. Those of you who work hard and do well in several subjects in school will eventually find your passion while you are in college. This is okay—because you will seize the opportunity at that time.

> You are entitled to nothing in this world other than opportunity.

You are entitled to nothing in this world other than opportunity. Despite family conflicts, poor parents, or a rough home life, you always have opportunity. The issue is what you do with that opportunity. You have every chance to begin creating a life of your own that starts in high school and continues through your college education. Consider networking with professionals in your field of choice and you can establish a career that can move you forward for a lifetime of success. Spread your wings and fly in a career that you choose on a journey all your own.

ALYSSA

Reach Your Potential!

Several years ago a student of mine was the senior class president, and with that comes the responsibility of giving the commencement speech. Alyssa was an exceptional student who was mature beyond her years. She wanted her speech to be different from those of the past. She gave it considerable thought, and went through draft after draft, hoping it would be memorable and applicable to all students as they pursue their plans after high school.

Alyssa stood before thousands of people and made her speech. It affected many people that day and I hope you find it memorable too. A portion of Alyssa's address follows:

. . . Lastly, the common cliché "spread your wings." This saying kind of compares us graduating seniors to birds, which works if you really think about it. But it doesn't specify what kind, and it doesn't indicate that you'll actually get airborne, or if you do, where you'll actually land, or that you will land safely. You may feel like a chicken, or a penguin, because spreading those wings doesn't seem to get you anywhere. The point is to wiggle those wingtips, especially if you feel a bit let down after graduation. It may not make you feel like a soaring eagle, but that is not necessarily a bad thing. You didn't fail. Remember graduates, you are entering a society with multiple challenges and obstacles to over- come, so don't be too hard on yourselves. But don't let that be an excuse; wiggle those feathers and wiggle them often. Perhaps we won't "spread our wings" like we thought we would. Graduates, you spreading your wings allows you to fly wherever you choose. Your wings are your own wings. They're something that you are born with. Allow them to take you on a journey all your own. Your flight path is wherever you make it, and today you have a diploma to take you there.

So, Class of . . . , let us spread our wings. Let us fly. Let this next stage of our lives be the best time in our life and let's do it with the people sit- ting next to us today; the ones that we will see again down the road. I wish you all the best of luck. And again, congratulations graduating class of . . . !

Alyssa's speech speaks of the challenges that face graduating seniors as they enter college and the work force. You must be will- ing to spread your wings, however humble, and explore opportu- nities that can help you in the future. You must take calculated risks and be willing to work hard and, when it comes time to look for a job, network with other professionals.

> You must take calculated risks and be willing to work hard and, when it comes time to look for a job, network with other professionals.

EMMA

Stand Out from the Crowd

Other students have taken a more direct route to planning their future. Emma was a student of this caliber. She wanted to work hard. She wanted to achieve. Why? Because she knew that she was able to reach her career goals. She recognized that she was the only person who was able to unlock her own ability. Emma aspired to be an architect. She had long dreamed of taking an idea in her head and turning it into a functional building where people could live, work, and play. Too many students don't have dreams; they just take things day by day. When you do this, however, you eventually realize that years have passed but you are essentially in the same place—only older. If a student has a dream it becomes much easier to assist them in coming up with goals or stepping stones so they can actually reach them.

Emma was a solid student who worked hard. She had about a 3.4 grade point average and earned a score of 24 on her ACT. She was solid academically, but by no means was she naturally bright or gifted. She worked hard and was willing to take the necessary steps to stand out from others as she pursued her high school education.

Architecture is a highly competitive field; Emma wanted to take steps to establish her career in high school, so she took college classes through a dual enrollment program to help her stand out. This program allows a student to take college classes at no cost at area colleges and universities. This was important because it helped Emma begin the process of networking with her college professors, which helped in her transition to the university a year later when her application was accepted. Emma didn't settle with just taking college courses. She took advantage of an opportunity and followed that up by interviewing someone who had his own architectural firm simply because she was given his contact information by a friend.

The interview was invaluable, and allowed Emma to ask many questions about what it was like to work in the architecture field. Emma asked questions about how he got started, how many years of schooling he needed, and where he worked when he was just out of school. He showed her completed drawings and told her about the various projects he was working on. This was an opportunity that she could have declined for any number of reasons. She could have said, "I am not ready for this," or "I'm too scared," but she embraced the chance and was rewarded for it.

It is important to realize that this world owes you nothing. Often, we are given a hand up by someone—which is always far more valuable than a handout. There's an old proverb that says: "Give a man a fish and you feed him for a day. Teach a man to fish and you feed him for a lifetime." You need to recognize chances and run with them, as Emma did, even if you are scared of failing. You are guaranteed to fall short if you don't even try. Emma didn't know it at the time, but while she was interviewing the architect, she herself was being interviewed and evaluated by him. It turned out that the architect was looking for an intern, someone who could assist with the day-to-day operations of the architectural firm. When Emma found out, she was elated and recognized how valuable this would be. She worked with the architect for the summer prior to leaving for college. She still keeps in contact with him and is using that

> There's an old proverb that says: "Give a man a fish and you feed him for a day. Teach a man to fish and you feed him for a lifetime."

experience and contact as a means to network for a future internship or potential job.

On the outside Emma looks like a typical high school student who had solid grades, got some breaks in her career planning, and ran with those chances. I share Emma's full backstory so you can fully appreciate how far she came.

Emma's mother was a seventeen-year-old high school student when she became pregnant. Throughout the pregnancy, she had been planning to put Emma up for adoption once she gave birth. She went through numerous applications of potential adoptive parents and finally, after much contemplation, decided on who was going to adopt and raise her child.

Emma was born at the end of May, just ten days before her mother graduated from high school. Emma's mother held her newborn daughter to say goodbye, but with each passing moment she grew apprehensive about giving her baby up for adoption. She so wanted to do the right thing, both for the baby and for herself, and knew this would be a decision that would affect the rest of her life. In the midst of tears her mom prayed and asked God for a sign. Just then, baby Emma opened her eyes and seemed to stare right into her eyes. That look was enough to convince her mother to keep Emma and cancel the adoption arrangements, despite the knowledge of how crushed the adoptive parents would be.

Emma's dad left immediately. Baby Emma and her mother lived with her grandparents. Emma's mother later married, but he ended up having an affair so her mom and stepdad got divorced when she was eight. Again, they moved back in with her grandparents. Emma has never had a father to speak of. She and her mom had to make it on their own, luckily with the unconditional support of her grandparents.

So by no means did Emma have it easy. She learned the hard way that you have to keep working, no matter the odds, or how big the curveballs life inevitably throws your way. She realized growing up that there are no handouts in life. She understood that if opportunity comes you need to grab it, because if you don't, someone else will. Against all odds, Emma established her career and overcame obstacles to succeed. You can, too, if you have the desire to reach your true potential.

Almost daily, students come into my office and let me know that they have no idea what they want to do with their lives. Beyond classes and credits as it relates to graduation, I spend a large majority of my time working with students about plans for college, but more specifically their plans for establishing a career.

Many students are afraid and reluctant to choose a career direction. Fear paralyzes them because they do not know what they want to do for a career, or because they are afraid of making the wrong career choice. As much as they want to leave the walls of their high school, these same walls have become a source of security for them.

I have had countless students over the years who tried—knowingly or unknowingly—to sabotage their high school graduation and career plans. Blake was one of them.

BLAKE

Making the Most of a Second Chance

I had Blake come to my office numerous times. He was a senior who struggled to perform in the classroom. This was not because of a lack of ability, but instead because of a lack of effort. I continued to work with Blake on a fairly regular basis. Sometimes he would come down and see me, and other times I would call him out of class in an effort to assess his academic progress. Unfortunately, our meetings often became a conversation about his lack of progress and lack of effort.

What Blake didn't know was that I had been speaking with his father on a regular basis. I tried just about every approach, idea, and intervention I could think of to motivate Blake to succeed and graduate on time. His dad and I strategized about ways that he could help his son and keep him accountable at home. Eventually, I reached a pivotal point with his dad. He was done trying. He was out of ideas and believed that he had done all he could do to help his son. Seeing nothing in return, he gave up. This made things extremely difficult for me because it seemed that the further we got into the second semester and the closer it got to graduation, the less Blake was willing to do.

With his dad's approval, I continued to see Blake, striving to motivate him to care, to take an interest in his future. On one particular day, Blake finally arrived from English class, closed the door and sat down. It took him far longer than it should have, and I believe he took his time to let me know he was upset with me. I was constantly striving to hold him accountable for his attitude and lack of effort.

I told Blake that we had reached a critical stage as it related to graduation because it was the end of March, with the ceremony just about three months away. You either have to step up, take responsibility, improve your grades, and get your diploma, or don't graduate and accept the consequences of your choices and lack of effort. I vividly recall telling him something that has stuck with me over the years, and a piece of advice that I have shared with numerous students as time has gone on. I told Blake that I believed in him more than he believed in himself. I told him that he could choose not to graduate. He could delay the responsibility of growing up and being an adult, but that he could not avoid it. I encouraged him to take control of his life and his future by thinking of a career that he was interested in.

"Blake, what are you interested in?" I asked.

He responded, "criminal justice."

"Interesting choice; why criminal justice? Why not something else?"

"Well . . . as you know, I have had some legal troubles of my own over the years, with underage drinking; helping others is what I want to do . . . besides, it kind of helps make up for some of my past mistakes."

I tell my students to find something that they would love doing, and then come up with a plan to find someone to pay them to do it. For some, it's medicine, law, education, or construction work as a career. For Blake it was criminal justice. I sent him back to class with one last thing to ponder.

I said, "Blake, if you can't avoid growing up, and you can't avoid the responsibility that comes with it, then wouldn't it be wise if you took advantage of being able to control where you will end up?" With that thought Blake agreed that he would at least think about what I said. I said "Great!" and was encouraged by his response. His attitude had changed. He seemed to have a different look in his eyes. I sent him back to class telling him that if he wanted my help on this journey to let me know because I would *support* him through his classes, graduation, and college; I just would not do it *for* him.

The next day, Blake came to my office with a renewed attitude. His perspective had changed. He thanked me for not giving up on him, and with that we established a plan of what he needed to do to graduate and prepare for college.

Blake changed his attitude, and made up whatever assignments he could. He was always in class, never missed an assignment, and stayed focused on what he had to do. He had a very poor ACT score, which I knew would cause him to be denied admission to college. I contacted the university asking them to consider accepting him on a conditional basis by placing him on academic probation. Several weeks went by and he was accepted on the conditional basis that I requested. He passed all of his classes—barely, but he passed—and walked proudly across the stage at graduation on the first Saturday in June.

Once Blake graduated, that was the last I heard from him. I often wondered how college went for him. Did he succeed? Did he drop out? Did he make it?

One June day several years later I received an email from his father.

> *Dear Sir,*
>
> *I hope this email finds you well. I wanted to give you an update on my son. Blake graduated with a degree in criminal justice . . . and immediately started his master's program . . . He is clerking for a law professor this summer . . . and he has also been hired to be a grad assistant for the school year starting in September. He is prepping for his LSAT test for admission into law school. His grade point average was a 3.9 for his semester in grad school and he finished with a 3.8 in undergrad school. He made the National Honor Society and all of his professors gave me very high reviews of Blake as a person and as a student. He has come so far and has become a fine gentleman as well as a student.*

Mr. K, Blake and I are so aware that this was made possible because of you and your commitment and time you put in the future of Blake and you never gave up even though you were pushed to the limit. You obviously are in your profession for the betterment of kids and for their potential. You are a hero in our eyes and words cannot express our thankfulness for your time and effort you forwarded Blake.

I hope in the future when you have these special situations at your work that you can reflect on the success of Blake and you can find the effort and passion for your students in the future that you forwarded to Blake. You have a talent, sir, to put your ego on hold for your students and their well-being; you are an example for all teachers and counselors in your profession. You have made a difference and I congratulate you in your success. . . .

When Blake graduates with his master's and his entrance into law school next year I am going to have a very nice party for him at a local restaurant to celebrate his success and we would both be honored if you and a guest would attend. It would be an honor to have you there.

In closing, we just want to thank you again, and if there is anything I can ever do for you, speak on your behalf or whatever I can be of any assistance to you, please don't hesitate to contact me.

Sincerely,

Tom (Blake's dad)

I have seen in my career that there are many students who don't have the successful outcome that Blake did. He is the exception to the rule. After years of avoiding school and academics, Blake wanted to take hold of his future; this came about through his desire to establish his career and follow the dreams that were unlocked, in part, when we spoke in my office.

I enjoy finding out about my former students. I always wonder what paths their lives took. Did they take control of their life or did they let it control them? I knew Blake had made progress and was heading in the right direction, but I was thrilled to recently receive this additional email from Blake's father. It really showed me that Blake had found his passion, and will be a positive person both in his career and in society as a whole.

Sir,

It has been a long road with a very happy ending. My son Blake found out yesterday that he passed the bar exam on his first attempt. He now has a bachelor's in criminal justice, a master's in criminal justice and homeland security, a law degree from the university he attended, and now just passed the bar exam.

As we know, Blake had many issues as a high school student, a polite way of saying an attitude problem. He had much difficulty with his parents' divorce. Many teachers gave up, but not you. You did not accept the old excuse . . . well, many kids are from divorced families. You treated Blake with a firm hand but a concerned hand as well. You are responsible for him getting into college where he blossomed and matured. He was even a graduate assistant at his university, can you imagine that? He interned the last few years with the ATF federal agency and also at the defense attorney's office with the department of legal aid. He is entertaining job offers and there is no doubt he will be a positive member of society. In the next few months I will be having a party to celebrate Blake's accomplishments and would love for you to attend.

Please, in the future, when you are having a bad day or some kid is driving you nuts, or this kid feels that there is no hope for himself, remember Blake. You changed his life, you made a difference. That is why I know you went into the field you have chosen. Congratulations sir, you made a difference in my son's life and I will never forget you. Please pass this letter on to your superiors, or display in your office. I hope this can be viewed as a trophy on your mantel.

Sincerely,

Tom (Blake's dad)

I don't take credit for the successes of my students or the responsibility for their setbacks or failures. Blake achieved because he wanted to. Each of my students has this opportunity. *You* have this opportunity. The question is, will you take hold of it? Blake realized that he wanted to establish a career in criminal justice. He took the hard path to get there, but he achieved his goals. You have the opportunity to plan for your future just like Emma and Blake did. It's never too early to start planning, but also never too late to get back on track. Set a goal and take small, realistic steps to get there.

Think seriously about what you want your career to look like. Planning for a career through discussion, collaboration, and networking allows for your career plans to come into focus. The fear is minimized while the plan to achieve it becomes realized. The job market is tight. The competition is great. At some point you have to spread your wings and fly, as Alyssa wrote. The flight toward a successful career is made much easier with a flight plan. Make a career plan, break it down into a manageable series of steps to achieve it, and rest assured that your career flight will be comfortable and the landing smooth.

> Planning for a career through discussion, collaboration, and networking allows for your career plans to come into focus. The fear is minimized while the plan to achieve it becomes realized.

POINTS TO PONDER . . .

✔ You are entitled to nothing in this world other than opportunity. What plan have you created to help you establish a career?

✔ What are your career plans? How hard are you willing to work to achieve a successful career? After all, countless people will be trying to obtain the same job you want.

✔ What are the skills you need to excel in the career of your choice? Do you have those skills? If not, how are you going to obtain them, or do you need to reconsider your career interests?

✔ What professionals in your career path can you begin networking with now in an effort to help you on your journey? Whom would you contact?

✔ There are no handouts in the world of work. What skills do you have that set you apart from others?

✔ You can *delay* growing up, but you cannot *avoid* it. Planning for a future career minimizes the amount of fear you may feel about establishing one.

✔ Not everyone will help you with your efforts, and some might even try to steer you the wrong way. Remember, this is *your* life, and *your* future. Work hard and don't allow others to lead you in the wrong direction.

Part III

TIPS TO SUCCEED

Chapter 13

PROBLEM SOLVING

To succeed in this world, you must have the ability to solve problems. Problem solving is using your ability to come up with an effective solution when you are unsure of what to do. When you learn how to solve problems, you can depend upon yourself to get through challenging situations when you have no one around to advise you.

Behind closed doors, I meet with students to discuss a variety of issues and difficulties. I may ask a student why he did not do his homework, or another why she is failing a class. I ask these

> Problem solving is using your ability to come up with an effective solution when you are unsure of what to do.

questions on a daily basis, and more often than not the response I get is "I don't know." "I don't know" is *not* an answer; it is an excuse and a means to *avoid* giving an answer.

> "I don't know" is *not* an answer; it is an excuse and a means to *avoid* giving an answer.

It's a much better idea to admit that you have made a mistake, or have an issue, and then take the right steps to move forward. It takes far more energy to avoid something than it does to tackle it head-on, even if at first it might seem overwhelming or frightening. Problem-solving allows you to celebrate your successes while being honest about those areas where you are lacking. No one is perfect; everyone has some area where they fall down. When we work to solve our issues, we strengthen our weak points and round off the rough spots that each one of us has. If you are able to face your shortcomings you are well on your way to succeeding in school—and in life. By the way, if you can do this, many adults would be impressed!

While some teens grow up with little to no adult support, many others have been raised in a world where people—parents, relatives, friends, coaches, etc.—have tried to eliminate the turbulent times in their lives.

I recognize the benefits of this—and certainly parents and other concerned adults should protect children from danger. But in other situations, where there is no real threat, this ultimately leads to minimizing life's struggles. Maybe it's a mother who saw her daughter stressed about her looming science project deadline, and "helped" her by doing most if not all of the work so her daughter could hang out with her friends instead. It could be another mom who—after hearing from other parents how much easier it is—pays a private psychologist nearly a thousand dollars to test her son into the school's gifted program, after he didn't meet the school district's diagnostics. When the son struggles with the difficult classwork, she pays for a team of tutors to help him keep up.

Or maybe it's a dad who talks to the varsity basketball coach about his son's lack of playing time, when he knows the boy seldom goes to practice.

Having someone take away the difficult, "bad" times in your childhood and teenage years, in reality, only hurts you in the long run. If your mother did your school assignments when you were young, you will not be able to handle more complex work as you get older. You certainly can't take your mom to college with you, even if she wants to go! If you get put in accelerated classes in elementary school that are too difficult for you, you will not learn the basics well and may stumble when you get to higher levels in middle and high school when grades *really* count. If your dad talks to the basketball coach so you can play in the game and lets you off the hook for practice, you will never learn the importance and value of training and preparation, and how they promote a "team" concept. As can be said in all these cases, you will never learn the ultimate, long-term lessons of perseverance and the self-esteem building rewards of working on something to the best of your ability.

We learn from what we go through; it makes us stronger and more resilient. We learn through what we experience; that is what creates our life story. We even learn through bad times. A bad grade received because you chose to play video games instead of studying for your test; a relationship broken because you kissed another girl at a party when you thought no one would notice; a true friendship lost because you decided to hang out instead with the "popular" girls—who then dump you—all become learning opportunities. Sometimes

> We learn through what we experience; that is what creates our life story.

these things hurt, but in the end they make you better equipped to handle complicated issues in your life. These experiences define who you are and what you value.

> We learn through experiences, both good and bad, and it is those experiences that teach us how to cope and manage stress and loss.

We learn through experiences, both good and bad, and it is those experiences that teach us how to cope and manage stress and loss. Coping skills to help you deal with a crisis are great, but you also need to have insight and the perspective to realize that difficulty and struggles are a part of life. Being sheltered or protected from everything only does you a disservice. Accepting that life can be difficult is what sharpens you and makes you better as a person. Dealing with setbacks shapes you. It won't hurt you in the big picture. Dealing with struggles gives you opportunities to problem-solve and aids in your preparation for a life of your own, where the protective guard of parents is replaced by self-reliance.

Your ability to problem-solve can be tied directly to your level of personal responsibility. I am a big believer in being accountable. If you are irresponsible, it causes someone else to care for you. Many would prefer that. They want someone else to take care of them and make decisions for them. It is certainly much easier this way, and if something goes wrong, they can lay the blame on the person or people who made the decision. They don't ever really appreciate the difficulty of doing the work, solving a problem, or even having compassion for others who do. You may have this view, and I hope that you come to realize how shortsighted it is.

As you get older, you'll see that this is where people begin to separate themselves from the pack in college and in the work force. There will always be people who only want to put forth minimal effort. If you go this route, you won't have to work as hard. Chances are, however, that you probably won't be able to reap the rewards of a better job, whether that means more money, or nicer working conditions. Strive to develop skills to solve problems. Find a way out of a problem by coming up with an appropriate solution. Those of you who can problem-solve can go places in life. You can have a job in the future that has the perks of a quality salary along with benefits that provide security for both you and your family. If unexpected difficult times come, like a layoff or some other unexpected job loss, you'll have the skills to find another source of employment.

Many of you have grown up in the era where we don't want anyone's feelings to get hurt, or to feel inferior to others in a group. If you played youth sports or were involved in other activities, likely everyone on the baseball team got a trophy, everyone at the dance recital got a ribbon, and everyone who ran in the race got a medal. Everyone was recognized and everyone was equal. So it was probably a shock when you got older and suddenly everything got very competitive, seemingly overnight. School sports teams have tryouts, make cuts, and then select only the most skilled players to play in the games. Students with the highest grades get recognized for their academic success at an awards ceremony and are rewarded with certificates recognizing them for their achievements. The reality is that we are not equal. There is no trophy for all and certainly no quality paying job for all. Problem-solving and a strong work ethic are the keys to success.

Problem-solving takes many forms in life. It is not just related to schoolwork or in your career. It can be as simple as needing to print a paper and your printer jams, or needing a pen to take notes in math class but not having anything to write with.

For some, the problems can be much larger and have increased significance. They did for Zack.

ZACK

If Only I Could Have Picked My Parents

Zack was a junior in high school. He seldom showed up at school and, as expected, he floundered academically and got poor grades. He was already on the verge of not graduating because he failed too many classes his *freshman* year. It was possible that I would have to recommend him for an alternative high school where he could earn more credits faster so he could graduate in a timely manner. These schools are designed for students who are deficient in credits and become a last resort for struggling students. Smaller class sizes, greater accountability, and a rigid attendance policy are interventions that provide support for these students to finish high school on time. I called Zack out of math class to discuss the gravity of his situation. I'd been through similar conversations with many students before, so I assumed I would be sharing what I knew about problem-solving with him. I was taken by surprise, however, when this student taught me a few lessons!

Zack appeared nervous as he walked into my office, closed the door, and sat down. I think he knew that I was calling him down because of his grades. The look on his face was one of desperation and hopelessness: desperate because he wanted to finish high school; hopeless because he had no idea how he was going to get there.

Given his facial expressions, I asked in an upbeat tone, "Hi Zack! How are you?"

"Okay," he responded.

"You don't look okay . . . what's up?" I asked.

Zack stared at the floor, then as he fidgeted in his seat said, "Nothing."

"If you're willing to share with me what's going on, I'm willing to listen." I said. His body language and demeanor told me that he had a lot he was holding back. He just needed permission and a safe environment to share it.

"I know why you called me down," he said.

Compassionately, I asked, "Why?"

Zack responded, "You see my grades and credits and you notice that I am in danger of not graduating, even now with two years of high school left."

"Zack, you're right. What's going on? You are a bright student."

"My home situation has not been good."

"Okay . . . what do you mean by that?" I said.

"My parents have a lot of problems. They don't get along. They argue a lot and their drinking problems do not help anything. Besides, my dad is likely going to jail again. They embarrass me, but I am just about done dealing with this."

"What are you going to do? I asked curiously.

He said, "A couple of months ago I asked my aunt and uncle if I could live with them . . . permanently."

I answered, "That is a big step. What did they say?"

"Mr. K, they were excited about it. They were more than willing. In fact, they met with my mom and dad, and my parents were excited to give me up! I know . . . sad isn't it?"

"I guess I know why school hasn't been your priority," I said.

"Yeah, you're right. Everything should be official at our court date tomorrow and then I can put all of this behind me."

He was quiet for a few minutes, but I could tell he wanted to say more because he started fidgeting with the zipper on his backpack. He looked up at me, took a deep breath, and said, "Mr. K?"

"Yes Zack."

"I need your help with one thing now that I am going to start living with my aunt and uncle."

"What's that?" I asked.

"Mr. K, I really want to graduate. I know it does not look good for that to happen, but I am in a better place now. Can we make a plan for graduation to happen?"

Once Zack's living arrangements became official the next day, he and I sat down together, trying to map out a plan to see if he could graduate without having to transfer to an alternative school. His plan would consist of a correspondence class and multiple summer school classes. This would only work if he got passing grades in all of his classes for the next two years.

Zack was faced with a problem. He was in dire circumstances and accepted the fact that he needed a new living arrangement in order for him to have a better chance at being successful. Instead of giving up, he stepped up. Using his creativity, self-reliance, and determination, he faced the problem head-on and devised a solution. Instead of quitting, he rose to the challenge. He could have chosen to wallow in his misery, complain constantly, blame his parents, and accept his fate of likely not graduating—but not Zack.

Zack completed the correspondence class, excelled in the summer school classes, made passing grades in every class, and walked across the stage at graduation two years later. His aunt and uncle gave him the stability he so desperately needed. I'm sure he had his weak moments, but in the end Zack was a fighter and a problem solver. He was resilient. He wanted to better his life and was willing to do whatever was necessary to make it happen and succeed. He did not let an obstacle impede his progress in life.

Sadly, his parents rarely spoke to him again, and it wouldn't surprise me if they missed seeing him reach his goal of graduating. We can speculate as to why, but they wouldn't give him any reasons to explain themselves. While it must have hurt, it nonetheless validated for Zack that he did the right thing, just like Sydney.

SYDNEY

Friends to the Rescue

Sydney was a freshman girl and the only child in her family. She was social, confident, hardworking, and intelligent, to name a few, and with all of these great qualities had all of the potential in the world. Most parents would be proud of a child who exhibited character traits such as these, and would want her to be accepted by her peers. Moms and dads often go to great lengths to help their children succeed, sometimes sacrificing their own wants and needs to help them.

It's certainly not unusual for a student to be verbally harassed by other students who are jealous of their accomplishments, and in that case the student would typically seek comfort, support, and safety at home. In Sydney's case, however, it was the opposite; the taunts she received were from her own parents. According to Sydney, they were often envious of her and belittled her. Throughout her middle school years and into high school, she dealt with cutting comments from them. To make matters even worse, they started picking out what she was going to wear each day to school. She had no say in the matter and they consistently laid out clothes on her bed that were wrinkled, unkempt, dirty, and oftentimes didn't even match. She was embarrassed but students were kind to her regardless of her appearance. Sydney never reported any instances where harassment or bullying was a problem from her peers. Her parents did not go to college and, strangely enough, resented her ability to go and make a better life for herself. She was also well-liked and they were jealous of her friendships. I believe they wanted to sabotage those relationships, believing that if she did not dress well no one would talk or hang out with her. Sydney had a problem and needed to be a problem-solver.

People will treat you however you let them.

In working with thousands of teenagers over the years I have learned, for the most part, that people will treat you however you let them. This holds true for you now and will still be true when you are an adult. You have to set a boundary with people even though you will always have people who will be rude. Doing this lets others know where you stand as to how you want to be treated. If you don't like how someone is treating you, then you need to change something. Sydney could have chosen to sit in her room with the door

If you don't like how someone is treating you, then you need to change something.

closed and cry about her circumstances. I am sure she probably did do this at times, but she realized that this would get her nowhere. If she did this, she would forever be a victim. At some point, she needed to take action and, in the end, decided she was not going to let her parents limit her happiness.

The humiliation of the dirty, mismatched clothes was an everyday occurrence that lasted almost six weeks before Sydney got to a point where she could not deal with it any longer. You can hardly do your best in class when you look and smell bad. Sydney needed a coping strategy to regain her own personal power. Using her wits and her close relationships she came up with a brilliant solution. Sydney would get up in the morning and wear what her parents demanded. They would drop her off at school where she'd meet one of her friends in the bathroom. The friend would have an extra set of clothes in Sydney's size for her to change into before the first bell rang, and that is what she would wear for her day at school. At the end of the day, she would change back into the clothes her parents picked out for her. Her dad picked her up from school completely unaware of the switch.

Each day, a different friend would bring clothes in for her. She asked multiple girls for help because she did not want to burden any one person with this task. The plan worked like a charm. She loved all the clothes she got to wear! This routine took place every day of the school year—for nearly two years—and her parents never knew this took place.

Sydney had a problem and came up with a solution. She did not allow her circumstances to define her; instead, she rose above them and forged her own path to happiness and pride in herself. It's sad that she lacked the love of her family, but she discovered tremendous love and support from her many friends. If she could get through something like this, she could overcome most anything.

> Life is not about the problems but how you respond to them.

Life is not easy. Problems are a part of life just like they were for Zack and Sydney. Life is not about the problems but how you respond to them. Is there a problem you are having that seems impossible to conquer? How does it make you feel? Helpless? Defeated? Powerless? Now consider what your life would look like if you *embraced* that problem and solved it instead of viewing it as an obstacle that can't be overcome. Even if you don't have your license yet, you will always be the driver of your own life. Put that problem in the rearview mirror by moving forward.

Sometimes students who want to be more independent and to solve their own problems flee from facing their problems head-on for fear that they will make mistakes and make circumstances worse. Unless it is something extremely significant where you must reach out to someone for help or advice, I encourage you to stretch yourself. Push yourself. Go beyond the limits of what you thought

> Stretch yourself. Push yourself. Go beyond the limits of what you thought you could do or try.

you could do or try. Find out what you are really made of. I would rather you make a mistake (hopefully a small one) and learn from it. To have a problem or crisis in your life and not do anything is worse because problems not addressed only increase in severity with time. It becomes the response I talked about earlier. People say "I don't know" to avoid any responsibility. Take charge and strive to resolve what you can control in your life. Don't push them away. Don't sweep them under the rug. If you do, they come out the other side more complex and much more difficult to resolve.

If you want to be a problem-solver begin by accepting the responsibility that is yours. This can best be achieved by being willing to change. Change is related to results, and is associated with achievement and success. People don't want to change for the worse. They may make poor choices, but that is not where they want to remain. When people desire to change it is for the better. They want to improve their life. If you desire to change you may be more willing to embrace the problems in your life because the change you are about to create leads to solutions for problems and, ultimately, personal satisfaction. This is the satisfaction found in you taking responsibility for problems and coming up with solutions that are achievable.

Being a problem-solver can take you places in life. The workforce is looking for people—potentially for someone like you— who can see a need and fill it. Recognize a problem and offer a practical solution. Companies desire individuals who can collaborate with others and then make a decision to solve a problem.

Zack and Sydney were both problem-solvers. They were in a tight spot and could have chosen to panic or wallow in their misery. Instead, they took action. Practice your problem-solving skills. Don't make excuses. No one wants to be weighed down by difficulties. Turn those problems into challenges by being willing to step out from your comfort zone. If you try but fail, you can learn from

> Turn those problems into challenges by being willing to step out from your comfort zone.

that and see how much you can grow. Embrace the opportunity to make a change. When you desire change, you desire to better your circumstances. Embrace change and bring about the successful outcome that you desire.

POINTS TO PONDER . . .

✔ How can your problem-solving skills help you achieve the change you would like to see in your life?

✔ Why do teenagers seem to give up when a problem arises instead of striving to come up with a solution?

✔ Do you give up or do you seek to solve your problems?

✔ Is change in your life difficult to accept? If so, why? How does your desire to solve problems impact this?

✔ If you don't solve at least some of the problems in your life, what will your life look like?

✔ When you do homework and you don't understand something, do you give up, or do you come up with a solution to your problem? What are some possible options to solve this problem?

✔ Do you cause others to be responsible for you because you are irresponsible? What do you need to do to change this?

✔ Are you the type of person who always makes excuses for things? How can you change and not make excuses any more?

✔ How does a person become a problem-solver?

Chapter 14

WORK ETHIC

I've worked with thousands of students over the years with issues, problems, and tragedies that must number in the tens of thousands. It's been fascinating to see how they respond to crises, both those that are big and seemingly insurmountable, as well as those that are small. Some students seem to avoid their struggles while others are up for the challenge and ready to face them head-on.

If I had to pick one characteristic that can help a student through a crisis, it would have to be a work ethic. There is no substitute for it. Students are best able to overcome their circumstances through determination and perseverance. They must have a passion that says, "I'm not going to allow this situation to get the best of me." This characteristic is found in students who have the resiliency to work hard and not settle for "good enough."

Some people believe that resiliency is a gene or innate personality characteristic; you are born with resiliency or you aren't. I cannot debate the accuracy of that, but I do believe that apart from resiliency students can choose to want better for themselves. Too many times students let their circumstances get the best of them. It rules them to the point that they are controlled by their crisis instead of their desire to overcome it. Every once in a while you meet a student who is up against a wall, but they stare that adversity in the face with sheer determination to overcome it. Ola was a senior who definitely fit that category, and she even surprised me with her resiliency.

OLA

Handcuffs and a 4.0 GPA

Ola was a brilliant student who was also hard-working. You met her earlier in this book, in Chapter 8. I saw her hundreds of times over her high school career. We talked about everything in life from classes to relationships and, when her senior year came, college applications. She took the most demanding classes and excelled in all of them, maintaining over a 4.0 grade point average. We often talked about how to handle the stress of her rigorous course load and schedule, but one day she came to see me and I could tell that she was rattled about something else, something major. While I thought I knew Ola very well, I realized afterward she had kept a lot to herself, and I came away having the utmost respect for her.

Graduation was only a few months away when Ola came to my office. She closed my door, sat down, and started crying. What began with a few tears turned into sobbing, and then she could barely utter a word. She cried and cried. While I have had many kids crying in my office, I had never seen this side of Ola and I don't think I have had someone as hysterical in my office as she was that day. I knew immediately that this was a major crisis.

As you might recall, Ola was born in Albania and moved to the United States with her family when she was five years old. America was all she knew. She spoke flawless English, was an honor roll student, and after much effort on her part received an acceptance letter to the University of Michigan—one of the most prestigious and highly selective public institutions in the country—where she planned to study pre-medicine. She had aspirations of becoming a surgical oncologist. She had devoted herself to taking the necessary classes, achieving good grades, and getting high ACT scores to take the first important step in this career goal.

Ola wiped away her tears, and after her sobbing subsided, I said, "Are you okay?"

Ola responded, stuttering and crying again in a frantic manner, "No! No! No!" She continued, "There is something you don't know about me."

"What's that?" I asked.

Still crying, Ola said, "For many years now I have had to report to immigration services with my family as we are trying to gain United States citizenship."

"Okay . . ."

Ola continued, barely able to get out the next words, " . . . and . . . I am being sent on a plane . . . deported . . . back to Albania."

My response was silence. It doesn't happen often, but I was totally caught off guard.

For years, Ola and her family had been reporting to the United States Immigration and Naturalization Service (INS). They had to report every two to three months to show they were still working on their immigration case after an attorney had made a clerical error that led to their case being closed many years prior. This latest visit was supposed to be a routine appointment. Ola's assigned case officer had asked Ola and her mother to come in early in the morning to "update some information in the computer system." What happened next was anything but routine: Ola was immediately arrested and handcuffed to a chair. She was told she would be deported in less than a week, two months short of graduating from high school.

I was flabbergasted, as Ola shared through her tears that not only was she was handcuffed but she had to sit that way for six hours! She was placed in a lower-level hallway next to some offices then transported, in leg and handcuffs, to the local city jail. Ola shared with me the crippling fear, overwhelming stress, and crushing anxiety that she was dealing with. It was totally understandable that she couldn't keep her emotions in check. She felt hopeless, had no place to turn, and did not know what to do next. Apparently the immigration official assumed that she would run. They obviously didn't know Ola very well, because if they did, they would be certain she posed no flight risk.

After much confusion, questioning, and discussion along with the intervention of a local congressman, the officer who was in charge of Ola's case agreed to release her until her scheduled flight back to Albania once the authorities were convinced that she did not pose any threat. Ola was finally released after being detained in a jail cell where she sat for almost two hours.

I was not the only person shocked by this unfortunate turn of events. Ola was popular with her peers, well respected by adults and teenagers alike.

Ola had a crisis that threatened to derail her future. Everything she had worked so hard to get, and that her family had sacrificed for, was in danger of disintegrating. It was almost like the board game Chutes and Ladders, where your game piece is at the very top, just a few squares away from the final square, and then you roll the unlucky number that sends you down a chute to the very bottom. This, however, was not fun and games; this was real life, a tragedy from which Ola and her family might never fully recover if they left America.

Ola had a good cry about this in my office but, true to her nature, she persevered through her misfortune. The immigration officer who handcuffed her to a chair not only did not understand that she wasn't going to break the law, he also underestimated Ola's determination to stay in this country. She always believed that she was blessed to be in America. She never took it for granted, the way many native-born citizens do, and she knew she was in "the land of opportunity." She understood that her ticket to a brighter future was staying here in the United States, which increased the odds of her achieving her dreams.

Although you might read this story and think the circumstances sound extreme, I included it so that you might realize that Ola's story illustrates a model of drive, determination, and work ethic. Many teenagers believe that things should just be given to them, but not Ola. Ola knew the limited opportunities she faced if she was sent on a plane back to Albania.

I had worked with Ola on her applications for college, which included several essays. Below is another excerpt from one of them. It clearly shows Ola reflecting on the words of her mother and why her parents brought her to America.

> ". . . I look at you and I see your potential, your drive, and your ambitions. The thought of you not having ample opportunity to toil and rise to your fullest potential, the thought of you being oppressed into a complacent, clinical, cynical woman, the thought of you being robbed of your aspirations repulsed me. I brought you to a place where opportunity is plentiful. Nothing will be handed to you my daughter. Everything you hope to acquire you must earn. You determine how far you will go in life. No one can quiet your voice here, unless you let them."
>
> I stared at the warrior of a woman next to me—my mom. She had abandoned everything she had ever known for her ultimate cause—to liberate me from an oppressive culture, to provide me with the ability to work and make my mark on humanity, to change the world, if I dared to dream so big. Today, I desire to enter college with the intent to unveil my greatest potential, with the intent to enrich [this] university with my diverse qualities, and with the intent to change, even one small fraction, the world.

Ola understood the sacrifice her mother had made when she came to America. She had more drive and determination than most. She was not one who settled for "good enough"—ever. She wanted only the best, and surrendering to go to her homeland was not an option for her, even though with each passing day it was becoming more likely.

After speaking with Ola numerous times over a period of weeks I found out that Ola and her family were taken advantage of by an attorney in New York when they arrived in America. The family had reason to believe that everything was in line as it related to them gaining their United States citizenship, but that attorney had misled them over a lengthy period of time.

After meeting with Ola's family, I learned that their attorney had not filed a follow-up motion and their case had been closed. They had fought for years to reopen the case while they were in deportation proceedings, but this proved to be difficult. The attorney that had made that clerical error many years ago had sealed Ola's fate: a ticket back to Albania the following week.

Most people would have seen the writing on the wall at this point and given up. However, Ola wasn't one of them! If she was going to have to go back to Albania, she was going to go back on that plane knowing that she, her family, lawyers, and friends, all did everything they could to overturn the decision. They contacted the press and after she shared her story on the local news, the Office of Immigration and Customs Enforcement received negative backlash from the community. They reconsidered their decision and allowed Ola to remain in the country until graduation, two months away.

In class, Ola was one of those students who wasn't going to settle for a C when she knew she was capable of an A. Ola worked hard because she knew it determined her future opportunities in life. As a result, Ola and her friends began a campaign to keep her in the United States. It became a schoolwide effort including staff. People rallied behind her and her family because they knew it was the right thing to do. The goal was to collect one thousand signatures as evidence of support as she tried to get another extension to remain in the U.S. for another year.

> Success in life is accomplished through hard work; there is no substitute for it.

I am a big believer in personal responsibility. Success in life is accomplished through hard work; there is no substitute for it. If you want to achieve greatness, work hard and excel in school. Overcome your obstacles instead of using them as an excuse to quit. Press on. Press forward. You are "given" what you *earn* through your hard work in school, college, and career. If you understand this you are many steps ahead of most people. Why? Because too many people want free things. In actuality these handouts come at a price. Your ability to make your own way and support yourself is critical; otherwise you will always be at the mercy of other people—good and bad. Instead, you need to be willing to get your hands dirty, to put in the work necessary to become self-reliant. Invest through working hard and you will receive what is due to you—in school and in life. It may not happen as fast as you want, but in time it will occur.

Remember there is always somebody behind you who wants to take your place. They want your job, salary, benefits, perks, etc. Work hard because society will let you know that everyone is replaceable.

What happened to Ola? She and her community not only met their goal, but far exceeded it: they collected 15,000 signatures within a few weeks of launching her campaign and petition through social media and word of mouth. Ola's request to remain in the U.S. another year was granted through the support of a senator from Illinois and a senator from Michigan because of their belief in Ola and her desire to remain in America. She and her family still reside in Michigan and are so grateful for all of the support they were given. She is still following her dream of becoming a surgical oncologist. She is still striving to use her qualities to change the world—even if it is one small fraction at a time.

Isn't it amazing what work ethic can accomplish? Wouldn't it be interesting to see what *you* could really accomplish? Some people are afraid to take a chance or try something new because they have a fear of failure. Others might actually fear success if they overcame it because they recognize that another obstacle might lie ahead that they would have to face, which frightens them. Fear can be crippling but you can overcome it if you work through your obstacles. Make an impact. Give what people need. Get what you deserve because you worked hard for it. Leave a legacy through your efforts. After all, we are not remembered for the things we have accumulated over our lifetime; we are remembered for the impact we have made on the lives of people. You will never be disappointed by working hard and reaping the benefits, and will only have regrets for what you did not try to do.

> Fear can be crippling but you can overcome it if you work through your obstacles.

POINTS TO PONDER...

✔ Do you have a strong work ethic that enables you to realize your true potential in life? If not, what do you need to do to develop a better work ethic?

✔ Always work hard in school, your career, and in life. Never think you are irreplaceable in your job; everyone is replaceable. There is always somebody waiting to take your place.

✔ Success in life is accomplished through hard work. There is no substitute for it.

✔ Are you a person who makes excuses when obstacles come your way, or are you the type of person who is willing to step up to overcome them?

✔ Invest through hard work and you will receive what is due to you. It may not come as easy as you would like, but hard work pays off.

✔ Leave a legacy through your efforts and work ethic. It will inspire and motivate those you work with. Are you inspiring others?

✔ If you knew you wouldn't fail, wouldn't it be interesting to see what you would accomplish? Work hard and don't let failure be an option.

Chapter 15

AWARENESS

A key component to being successful in this world is being aware of what is going on around you—both in your community and the world. It is so easy to get caught up in our own "bubble" world. At some point there has to be a moment where we realize that there is more to life than us. We have to move beyond who *we* are, to who else and what else is out there.

> A key component to being successful in this world is being aware of what is going on around you.

Life is not just about us, it is about being part of a community and finding our place in the world. We create a healthy balance in our lives by having an awareness of others and what they face.

Sometimes your greatest joys in life are found in helping someone else be successful. Your happiness comes from knowing you helped them achieve it. Additionally, it

> Life is not about just us, it is about being part of a community.

increases your level of empathy, allowing you to realize that maybe your struggles are not as bad as you thought when compared to the needs of others. We are not defined by who we are; we are defined by who we become. Who we become is based upon our life experience, what we make of the life we have, as well as those we live life with.

JACOB

Sometimes You Don't Realize
How Good You Have It

On the surface Jacob was a very successful student. He was intellectually brilliant and had strong social skills, yet he struggled to deal with others who had different family dynamics and living arrangements than what he was accustomed to. Jacob was the type of person who usually focused on himself; he wouldn't let the needs of others get in the way of what he wanted to achieve or accomplish. I wanted to increase his awareness of those around him and share with him my belief that he had much to offer these students, especially his ability to help them with their academics.

Behind closed doors Jacob and I would talk often about his plans after high school. He desired to attend an elite university. Although he was naïve and unaware, one of his best traits was his willingness to be molded, and he was always willing to be involved.

I told Jacob that I was expanding a mentoring program that I had started the previous year, in preparation for the upcoming school year. The program would be called Club Connect, and would pair upperclassmen, acting as mentors, with incoming freshmen to help them adjust to the demands of high school, academically and socially. After hearing about the program Jacob eagerly joined and was ready to get involved.

Jacob was certainly a person I wanted in the program as a mentor, but I had other plans for him. I paired him up with a ninth-grader who didn't care about school, came from a broken home, and always seemed to have discipline issues. Although I wanted him to mentor other students, I wanted the life circumstances of his mentee to help Jacob become aware of what other students face.

Jacob was more than willing to take on the challenge and did a great job fulfilling the role of a student mentor. Through Club Connect he was able to see how other people live. He not only became more aware of the circumstances of other students, but he also became more thankful for his own family and living arrangements. As the program closed I called Jacob down to discuss his experience.

"So Jacob, what did you think of the mentoring program?"

Jacob responded, "Well, I was nervous, not because I didn't know what to do but because I didn't know how my mentee would respond to what I said."

"How did he respond? Did you make an impact?" I asked.

"Pretty good! He only failed one class and last year he failed five so it was successful."

"Do you still talk with him?"

"Yeah, we keep in touch by texting and say hello in the hallways."

"Great!" I said, and added, "Jacob, did you learn anything from your experience with mentoring a struggling student?"

Jacob shared, "Yes, a lot! I realized that kids come from all kinds of homes and it's tough for them to deal with. It made me

appreciate what I have at my home and that there is more to being
successful in life than being concerned about only me."

Jacob found value in helping others. He recognized that he could be a difference maker in someone's life and followed through to make that happen. I encourage you to seek out a program such as this in your school and if it doesn't exist, be the one to recommend it. You can be the catalyst that begins a new program and you can reap the benefits of it just like Jacob. It can open you up to another world.

Many times when I meet with students in my office, I encourage them to make sure they watch the news or read the newspaper on a daily basis. I know at your age you might not care about these news events, but doing this makes you aware of and allows you to form your own opinions on important issues that are taking place in your community, your state, and around the world.

Watching the news or reading the newspaper *does not* give you a better understanding of the world, necessarily, but it allows you to reflect on what you see and hear. How do you feel about children dying in Africa, corruption in local government, school violence, or a murder in your city? Does it matter to you? Do you care, or are you just going to live in a fog far from the realities of life?

Some may criticize this viewpoint, believing that, at your age, you should be sheltered from the evil and chaos in the world to ensure that you are not shaped by the moral decay of society. This perspective sounds great in theory, but it is not reality. You are inundated with the corruption found in society through music, media, and so much more. In addition, many of you have personal or family issues that have allowed you to, at a minimum, see a glimpse of the negative aspects of this world. To prepare you for the responsibilities of life, we must help you process the dynamics of this world. You must talk openly and honestly with your parents, mentor, or other trusted adult about what takes place in society. You need to be aware of the political unrest in other countries and the hopeless despair of those seeking food to eat and water to drink.

Talking about these newsworthy events, both good and bad, may be difficult, but it's necessary. If people are the problem with society, people can also be the solution. Being aware of the issues not only allows you to have more meaningful conversations, it allows you to be part of that change.

> If people are the problem with society, people can also be the solution.

This awareness is vitally important because it develops maturity. Teenagers are the future of our society and awareness can also allow you to influence your peers in a positive manner. Too many times, teenagers' focus on negative pursuits causes students to succumb to the rampant chaos of this world. Teenagers who develop awareness can positively influence others and turn the tide to developing a new generation of mature and responsible teenagers. Are you one of these?

Too often, people complain about their struggles. News flash: *everyone* struggles. You need to encourage yourself and your peers to have the fight, the scrappiness, to want better despite setbacks. You can provide this positive perspective to others. This influence can lead to you making an impact on someone's life. You could be the missing piece of the puzzle for someone who needs help gaining control of his or her life and planning for the future.

> You could be the missing piece of the puzzle for someone who needs help gaining control of his or her life and planning for the future.

POINTS TO PONDER . . .

✔ Having a level of awareness lets you keep yourself in check. It allows you to see that there is always someone better off, or worse off than you are.

✔ Life is not about "you"; it's about living with a community of people.

✔ If your peers accept you, you have an opportunity to influence them. What does this mean, and how does it impact how you live each day?

✔ Read the newspaper or watch the news so you can see what is going on in the world. Filter the information you read or hear so that you can form your own opinions about the issues raised.

✔ How does a level of awareness about your community and events around the world help you have a greater impact on those with whom you come in contact?

✔ It's easy to get consumed with your own life. How can you keep perspective and stay aware of the needs of others?

✔ How are awareness and community service related?

Chapter 16

PASSION

Beyond helping students with the typical academic and social issues, I often find myself discussing the "big picture" issues in life with them. Not the topics that might usually come to mind—working and making money to pay bills—but aspects of life that go much deeper. My ultimate objective is to have my students achieve beyond what they think they are capable of. Too many times students do not have long-range goals; they live for right now, and figure they will deal with tomorrow when it comes. I think a lot of this is because of the emphasis our society places on technology. Teenagers want results instantly; it's what they're used to. Unfortunately, this habit causes them to put off planning for their future. High school flies by and before you know it the future is now—today.

The first step to achievement is desire. This in turn creates passion to achieve more. Passion is simply what drives you in life.

What do you want to have happen? What do you want to achieve? What hopes and dreams do you have? What excites you or motivates you? What difference do you want to make in life? What do you want to be remembered for?

> Passion is simply what drives you in life.

It's important to do something in your life that you are satisfied with and proud of. I want my students to live life to the fullest and be exhausted as they grow old. There are different kinds of exhausted, and I don't mean "old and tired." I mean exhausted to the degree that you got the most out of life that you could. I want you to look at your future self, and envision yourself saying: Yes, I loved others! Yes, I gave back! Yes, I worked hard! Life is all about what you do with it. Pay it forward—invest in others because they invested in you. Fulfillment is one of those big picture issues I like to talk about, but it is neither mysterious nor unattainable. Being fulfilled results from the passion you have for getting the most you can out of life.

The airwaves are filled with so-called "reality" television—but television is not real life; it is merely a distraction from reality and the demands placed on our lives. In real life, people have responsibilities, appointments, and demands placed on them from their workplace, families, and friends. Life becomes what you make of it and is more rewarding when you achieve what you're working toward.

OLA

You Never Get Back a Lost Opportunity

You recall Ola, a student of mine who was passionate about her desire to stay in America, as well as both her college and career goals and aspirations. She always shared with me how much she loved science. I inquired about her career plans, as I do every senior, and she told me she wanted to be a surgical oncologist— cancer surgeon. We had many conversations about her dreams and aspirations. We debated and discussed different avenues as it related to life and what she wanted to get out of it. I encouraged her to define what she wanted; she would clarify her interests through discussion as we worked together for her to narrow down her possibilities. In an essay for her college applications she wrote about her career plans and aspirations for success:

> *I've asked myself the question "Who are you and what kind of legacy will you leave behind?" almost every day. Will I be content living on through my lineage, like most people? Will I feel fulfilled with a comfortable life with a comfortable mind-numbing career? No, I will not. I am determined to challenge myself, determined to seek a different type of immortality than most: giving my patients a second chance at life. I aspire to become a surgical oncologist, but more importantly, despite the seemingly endless obstacles in my way to do so, I intend to work for patients who cannot afford the astronomical costs that accompany life-saving surgeries, patients who often lose their lives merely because they cannot afford to obtain the medical treatment they deserve. My goal is not to increase the money in my bank account; my goal is to decrease the amount of preventable deaths merely due to economic status. How can I go to a high-paying job when I know there are single mothers wasting away in front of their children simply because they cannot afford the surgery that would enable them to raise their children? How can I go home to my comfortable home when I know that there are patients who are foreclosing on their homes due to surgical fees? I cannot. I will not.*

When I unveil my career choice to most adults, they tell me my dreams are unrealistic and unattainable. They are wrong. The medical world needs to change somewhere—this change can start with me.

Ola had a passion to want something better. She wanted this because she had heard stories from her mother about what life was like in her homeland of Albania. She heard about people struggling to find a decent-paying job, food to eat, or adequate housing. Medical care there is also not the quality you would find in this country and often unavailable; even when it is available, it is an expense most people can't justify. In this country, of course, Ola has seen how expensive our medical care is, especially for those without health insurance. Because of this passion, she did not just strive for a job that would simply make her a living. Yes, she wanted that, but she also wanted so much more. Ola's aspirations may be extreme to some, but that is what being passionate is all about. Her desire is to impact the world on a grand scale, yet she recognizes the task at hand and is willing to do it one person at a time.

What would you do in life if you knew you would not fail?

What would you do in life if you knew you would not fail? Think about that. What would you do if you knew you would succeed? What drives you? What are you passionate about? What inspires you? For Ola, it was becoming a surgical oncologist and helping those less fortunate. For you it might be law enforcement, teaching, or being an entrepreneur. Having a vested interest in one's life and profession is what passion is all about; it's the pursuit of excellence in one's vocation. It's the drive to succeed despite obstacles. Certainly we know that some people fail in that they won't meet their desires, whether it be personally or professionally. However, what makes passionate individuals unique is that they don't quit; they continue to seek their aspirations. They look at obstacles as only setbacks that can be overcome. Passionate people *will* succeed. It may look a little

> What makes passionate individuals unique is that they don't quit; they continue to seek their aspirations. They look at obstacles as only setbacks that can be overcome.

different than they thought, but they will make it. Drive and determination allows them to overcome these obstacles, and that ultimately makes the success that much more rewarding.

Your passion should be what causes you to get out of bed each day. It should be something that excites you. Your passion itself should motivate you because it allows you to have an impact and make a difference. Many teenagers do not know their passion; you may be one of them. This is not because you do not have a passion, it is because you have not yet discovered it. If this is you, it might be helpful to do this short writing exercise.

First, take a few minutes to slow down, find a quiet place, and make a list of things that you love to do now. We live at such a fast pace that we never take the time to stop and consider those things we do that we truly enjoy. I have a sign in my office that says: "Love what you do." Your passion must be something that you enjoy, that you find rewarding, that you truly love doing. An idea from this list can potentially become your passion in life. I often tell students to think of something that they love doing now, then to find someone to pay you to do it or something similar. This becomes an easy way to begin the process of finding your passion.

Next, make a list of those things you have not done, but you have always wanted to do. This second list allows you to consider those things that you might be passionate about even if you haven't given them a try. It may be that you have not tried them because of the expense, fear, time, anxiety, location, energy, or finding the right opportunity, to name a few. What matters is that you have a genuine interest. This list allows you to dream. It allows you to come up with those ideas that you enjoy but really haven't taken the time to think about and try out.

Finally, select one or two ideas off of each list and put them in order with the ones you are most interested in or curious about at the top. Seek out some opportunities to try out these newfound interests. It may be through job shadowing, networking, community service, etc. You will never know if it can be your passion if you don't take the time to investigate it. Once you have a leading interest, there comes a point where you must make a decision and go with it. Decide to claim it as your passion. Pour yourself into it! The more experience you have with it, the more you know if you have something that can be your passion long term.[5]

5 http://www.wikihow.com/Find-Your-Passion.pdf

One student who did this exercise determined that she wanted to help people who were hurting. This was at the top of her list. She decided a nursing career would be a great fit for her; she was compassionate, empathic, and loved the social side of being around people. However, after beginning college and taking nursing classes, she found out that she could not handle the sight of blood. She became nauseous learning to change a bandage on a healing wound and became dizzy even watching someone else do it. Just because you believe you are passionate about something does not mean your experiences with it will support your choice.

Remember your passion can change; it likely will. It changes because of your experiences as your place and role in life changes. Right now you are a high school student, a teenager. Later you will be a college graduate seeking to establish a career. As life progresses you may become a husband, wife, or a mother or father to children of your own. As a result of these life changes what you become passionate about changes. This continues in career and in your personal life.

Teaching someone to be passionate about something is not easy; in fact it may be impossible. Passion comes from within. It defines you. It is who you are. Passion leads to acceptance of your current circumstances in life and your willingness to succeed regardless of the situation. This acceptance leads to your ability to influence others. You can influence others for the better to move people forward or deter people and lead them in a negative direction. This should be important to you now because it defines who you are as a person. A passion to "better" the people around you will impact your friends, dating relationships, career, and interaction with coworkers. It will also impact how you deal with your family as roles change because of your growing up and potentially establishing a family of your own. Passion helps you move both yourself and others forward. It allows you to invest and reap the joy of helping others achieve. Passion is simply an awareness of life combined with a work ethic and an attitude that leads to success. Are you willing to be passionate enough to succeed in life, or are you going to settle for "good enough"? Good enough is mediocre. It's not even average, because passionate people don't settle for "okay." They expect more of themselves. They expect more out of life. Do you?

> Passion comes from within. It defines you.

POINTS TO PONDER...

✔ Passion is what drives you. What do you want to achieve? What motivates you? What hopes and dreams do you have?

✔ What makes passionate people unique is that they continue to seek their dreams despite obstacles. They look at problems as things that can be overcome. Is this you?

✔ Passion comes from within. It motivates and defines you. It allows you to achieve those things that others thought would be impossible.

✔ Passionate people don't settle for "good enough." "Good enough" is not even average. They expect more of themselves. They expect more out of life. Do you?

✔ Life is all about what you do with it.

✔ Passion helps you move both yourself and others forward. Do you help others achieve? Why or why not?

✔ Life becomes what you make of it and more rewarding when you achieve those things you work toward. Passion is what helps you see things through to the end so they are realized.

CONCLUSION

The teenagers who enter my office are from all walks of life. They come from a variety of family situations and have a wide range of academic abilities. A teenager may come from a stable home or one consumed by dysfunction and chaos. Those from a less stable environment usually struggle academically, have mediocre grades, or have even failed multiple classes. They often lack enough credits to graduate.

A more common occurrence I've seen over the years is the teenager who wants to do better, but can't see a way out to make it happen. He cares, he has a passion, and even has dreams for a brighter tomorrow but he doesn't know what to do next. It's like seeing the blue sky up above but being in a deep, dark pit with steep walls and no ladder.

To this teenager, I encourage you to start anew—it begins with an attitude, a mindset that you want to do better and you *can* do better. This can be achieved by first seeking to become a person of character and conviction. Remember, you can't change the past, but you can impact the future. That future begins *today*. A positive attitude and a belief that you can succeed can go a long way in making that success become a reality.

You can't change the past, but you can impact the future. That future begins *today*. A positive attitude and a belief that you can succeed can go a long way in making that success become a reality.

With a renewed attitude, take manageable-sized steps along your journey toward a future filled with opportunity. Begin small. It might be a conscious choice, a desire to focus and pay attention more in class, and to renew this choice each day. It also may be a step to seek out help from a teacher after school on a regular basis, or become courageous and ask a question in class. For someone else it may be as simple as taking the step to turn in all of your assignments in three of six classes this week and build from there. Set goals that are small and they will be easier to attain. It will allow you to see yourself making progress toward your ultimate goals and build your self-confidence along the way. This will instill a belief within you that you *can* accomplish anything if you have the drive, determination, and will to make it happen.

Students who can't see a way out may need a guide or mentor to help them map out a workable solution. Students who come from a dysfunctional home, have a parent with a substance abuse problem, who struggles to make ends meet, or who came to America from another country, are all individuals who can benefit from having a mentor. Seek out your counselor at school, or even an administrator or teacher. You may consider speaking with an extended family member such as an aunt, uncle, or grandparent. One or more of these individuals may qualify as a trusted adult who could mentor you, especially if they are people you look up to as role models. It is okay to ask for guidance. This allows you to learn from someone who may have walked down the same path that you are on. You may be able to use their experience and wisdom to get back on track.

Additionally, a mentor can be that person to guide you to success and release you from whatever is holding you back, whether it's self-destructive choices you've made, or trying to cope with the dysfunction within your home. Mistakes are a part of life. They are going to happen; we just hope you don't make big ones that affect your life forever. Knowing you are making mistakes and *not* fixing them, not taking steps to ensure they don't happen again, or not being willing to ask someone for help, only leads to more self-destructive behaviors.

This glimpse behind the closed doors of a high school counselor is exactly that—a glimpse. Every day is different and brings new challenges to face, address, and work through. For the teenagers who have chosen to read this book, whether by choice or because you were forced to read it, thank you. I value your time and your consideration of what I have written. Remember, behind the closed doors of my office, through the stories my students share, I see the world *you* live in and the challenges that make life difficult. I am a high school counselor. I am empathetic to the issues that teenagers across the country face: challenges of poverty, broken homes, a parent in jail, a lack of food, a parent who abuses you or won't speak to you, mental health struggles, learning disabilities, and many more. Life is a challenge. I have seen it and lived it with teenagers like you. We all have challenges. The issue is not how great your challenges are; the issue is how you choose to respond to them. You have a choice: either overcome your circumstances or let your circumstances get

> We all have challenges. The issue is not how great your challenges are; the issue is how you choose to respond to them.

the best of you. I believe in teenagers. I believe in you. I also believe you can teach adults a great deal.

Don't give in to the temptations of alcohol, sex, and drugs. Break free from abusive dating relationships and family breakdowns. Don't get swallowed up by the trials of life. You can realize freedom from these traps and seek a plan of solid academics, college planning, and career success. You are capable of much more than you think. You can accomplish more, achieve more, and become more than you realize. Please understand that many of you spend too much time dwelling on the struggles in your life and worrying about what is to come. You have many strengths. You are good at many things. You have numerous skills and talents that end up lost in the fog of life's struggles. Emphasize the positive in your life and believe you can achieve what you want. Don't settle for "good enough" or "mediocre," strive for excellence and the best grades you can possibly get. This results in developing skills that will allow you to flourish not just in high school, but in college and a future profession all of your own. Create a vision for yourself and set out on a course with the awareness, passion, and work ethic to achieve it. Find an adult that you can trust to guide you on your journey so they can celebrate the victories in your life with you. You can overcome. You will achieve. Why? Ultimately, because you want to, you want better for your life and have more opportunities; you just have to minimize the excuses and maximize the determination to get you there.

The reality is, life is about the choices you make, and all choices have consequences. Consider these consequences prior to making decisions, and hopefully they will lead you to make more informed choices. Be honest with yourself. Look at the possible consequences for your actions, for what they are and not for what you want them to look like. Have you ever noticed

> The reality is, life is about the choices you make, and all choices have consequences. Consider these consequences prior to making decisions, and hopefully they will lead you to make more informed choices.

you can't lie to yourself? You always know the truth about yourself unless you choose to avoid it. You might be able to fool or mislead others, but you know what the correct choice or decision is— it's just a matter of if you will do the right thing. Honesty with yourself and making the best choices can lead you out of the darkness and into a brighter future because it minimizes the consequences of poor decisions. Many teenagers that I work with are honest with themselves and despite past poor decisions, grab life with both hands and begin down a path toward opportunity.

You can make the right choices—even though sometimes it may be difficult to resist temptation from your peers to do otherwise. Never think you deserve less and never stop believing that you have what it takes to achieve greatness. You can succeed! You can overcome, be resilient and set yourself on a course leading to success. How do I know you can? Because you have chosen to hold this book in your hands and read it. It is my hope that it will help you to see the value in taking responsibility, and will lead to you setting goals for your life that you can attain. Once the first step to change your life is made, the rest of your choices and decisions begin to fall into place and are much easier to make. Be true to yourself and avoid making excuses for straying off course.

The fact is that it's tough growing up in our present-day culture. You are growing up in a society that has many families with both parents busy and working to make ends meet, a higher divorce rate, greater financial struggles, and an increase in moral decay. Parents and the environment you're raised in can be obstacles or aids to your success. Regardless, you still have responsibilities that you must face. You can delay facing life and the problems of life, but you cannot avoid growing up and living your life. If a problem exists you must deal with it. If the problem is people, then people have to be the solution. Caring, supportive people can be the catalyst that you need to help you be successful; however, there has to be a will from within *you* to change. Your generation is now and opportunity awaits you. Overcome obstacles in your life that are a roadblock to your success and celebrate those achievements now and for the rest of your life.

The last student has left. The office chair has been pushed in, the light has been turned off, and the counselor's door has been closed. So what did you learn? Where are you headed in life? Now is your moment. You can reach your goals. You can achieve. Why? Because you were born to succeed. The best is yet to come. You can become whatever you choose. It's your life. It's your future.

Email me at *achievegreatness2014@gmail.com*. I would love to hear how *you* persevered through your struggles to achieve greatness and realize the exhilaration of victory in your life.

INTERNET RESOURCES

The following is a list of some helpful websites to give you additional guidance and insight on some of the topics covered in this book.

Multi-Use Websites
www.gocollege.com
www.collegenet.com
www.collegexpress.com
www.collegeview.com
www.collegedata.com
www.collegeconfidential.com
www.collegehounds.com
www.collegeplan.org
www.ecampustours.com
www.collegeweeklive.com
www.zinch.com
www.schutor.com

College Applications
www.commonapp.org
www.collegeapps.about.com
www.princetonreview.com

College Selection
www.campusprogram.com
www.cappex.com
www.nacac.com/fairs
www.collegesource.org
www.petersons.com
www.mycollegeguide.org
www.nationalappcenter.com
www.theadmissionsoffice.com
www.liberalarts.org
www.christiancollegeguide.net
www.catholiccollegesonline.org
www.lutherancolleges.org

Testing
www.act.org
www.actstudent.org
www.collegeboard.org
www.nationalmerit.org
www.fairtest.org

www.kaplan.com
www.ets.org
www.number2.com
www.compassprep.com

Financial Aid
www.fafsa.ed.gov
www.pin.ed.gov
www.fafsa4caster.ed.gov
www.studentaid.ed.gov
www.coheao.org
www.eduaid.org
www.savingforcollege.com
www.salliemae.com
www.estudentloan.com
www.finaid.org
www.mappingyourfuture.org
www.moncy.cnn.com/pf/college/
www.collegemoney.com
www.studentloan.com
www.usbank.com/studentloans
www.upromise.com

Scholarships
www.fastweb.com
www.scholarships.com
www.scholarshiphunter.com
www.freescholarship.com
www.college-scholarships.com
www.scholarshippoints.com
www.fastaid.org
www.americorps.org
www.rhodesscholar.org
www.oxfordscholarship.com
www.truman.gov

Diversity
www.blackexcel.org
www.venturescholar.org
www.questbridge.org

Athletics
www.ncaa.org
www.naia.org
www.collegeprofiles.com

Majors
www.mymajors.com

Careers
www.careerplanner.com
www.virtualjobshadow.com
www.careerkey.org
www.medicaltrainingdirectory.com
www.culinaryed.com
www.gapyear.com
www.internweb.com
www.careercruising.com
www.stats.bls.gov

Test Strategies
www.ub-counseling.buffalo.edu/
    skills.shtml
www.ub-counseling.buffalo.edu/
    anxiety.shtml

Résumé and Essay Writing
www.collegegrad.com/resumes
www.1-2-3-resumes.com
www.owl.english.purdue.edu

Mental Health

www.aacap.org	American Academy of Child & Adolescent Psychiatry (AACAP)
www.psychiatry.org	American Psychiatric Association (APA)
www.schoolcounselor.org	American School Counselors Association (ASCA)
www.ashaweb.org	American School Health Association (ASHA)
www.smhp.psych.ucla.edu	Center for Mental Health in Schools
www.kidsmentalhealth.org	Center for the Advancement of Children's Mental Health
www.casel.org	Collaborative for Academic, Social and Emotional Learning (CASEL)
www.mentalhealthamerica.net	Mental Health America
www.nami.org	National Alliance on Mental Illness (NAMI)
www.nasponline.org	National Association of School Psychologists (NASP)
www.nctsn.org	National Child Traumatic Stress Network (NCTSN)
www.starr.org/training/tlc	National Institute for Trauma and Loss in Children
www.nimh.nih.gov	National Institute of Mental Health (NIMH)
www.healthysafechildren.org	National Research Center for Mental Health Promotion and Youth Violence Prevention
www.sswaa.org	School Social Workers Association of America (SSWAA)
www.samhsa.gov	Substance Abuse and Mental Health Services Administration (SAMHSA)
ww.sprc.org	Suicide Prevention Resource Center (SPRC)

REFERENCES

Edwards, Ashton. "Teen drug overdose deaths surpass car accident deaths in U.S." KFOR.com. http://fkor.com/2013/08/30/teen-drug-overdose-deaths-surpass-car-accident-deaths-in-u-s/ (accessed 2014).

Policy Holders of America. "The Report Card." http://policyholdersofamerica.org/pdf_public. (accessed 2011).

Sparks, Sarah. "Community Service Requirements Seen to Reduce Volunteering." Education Week.

U.S. Department of Education, National Center for Education Statistics. (2014). "The Condition of Education 2014 (NCES 2014-083), Institutional Retention and Graduation Rates for Undergraduate Students." http://nces.ed.gov/fastfacts/display.asp?id=40 (accessed 2014).

Wiki How. "How to Find Your Passion." www.wikihow.com/Find-Your-Passion (accessed 2014).